Walkways of the Sea

by

Stephen Francis Cosgrove

Last Laugh Productions
2025

Artwork:
all photos including covers by Stephen Cosgrove, except:
facing page to page 1: Image by Sam Potter at pixabay.com
p. 30: Image by Tom/Analogicus at pixabay.com
p.74: Image by imarketem at pixabay.com
p.146: Image by Thomas G at pixabay.com

www.lastlaughproductions.org
logo by Bradley Stockwell

for my mother

Edith Gretchen Cameron

Preface:

Dear reader!

This collection is a continuation of coast poems begun with *The Nearest Place Distant,* and I'm promising more after this. There's just something about Oregon's westmost land that won't let you go home. But California's northern coast is also a part of this book and the area surrounding Eureka is fascinating — a place where history vies with a time *before* history.

Humboldt Bay is like a giant lagoon, and the lagoons north of town are completely enchanting. This book features a long piece about Oregon's famous Cannon Beach. I wrote about it from the standpoint of age thirteen, when I first beheld it. I wanted to capture the wonder I felt arriving at that amazing expanse of shore that owes its unusual width to silt from the Columbia River. And, as I've expressed elsewhere, Cannon Beach and the entire littoral it is a part of, for me, truly became an obsession…only hypnosis might make it stop!

Table of Contents

THE PERFECT TRYST

It was a search for the perfect tryst
A place to be apart at Stone Lagoon
        and with all that wooded shore it was easy

There'd been a lull between storms
The interlude one of glistening mazes
        that were mossy
        hierarchic

A rain forest waiting on obsession
Waiting   wet   for a tent   or shelter-half

Let the hideaway resemble a villanelle
And have enough structure to sing itself to sleep

Let rage and politics stand by
        and not enter into this Hindu setting

For we know that Everywhere is waiting
        on some mischief or other
That Everywhere will pause
As if absolute zero were its new best friend
        and wanted no temperature
        no heat
                to worry perfection

Think of all the damage
        that stays at home
                and stays out of Stone Lagoon

The lovers will eschew graffiti
And write new chapters for *Tristan and Isolde*
No one will care
        they've been subsumed in nineteenth
                                century foreplay

There will be a miracle unless the universe quits
There will be the sweetest kisses
        and the mind made a part of it
There will be the practice of the art of circumstance
All the cunning that instinct instructs

throughout the first four dimensions and counting

Their acts shall be day-for-night and vice versa
The spirit left to multiply its gifts
        and survive in a million unexpected ways

Where the channel joins sea to lagoon
And three solitary stones lean
        somehow remnant
                is a commingling
                not unlike the alchemical charge
                        that affections enact

They lay down   no goodness to estrange
Hands   just hands
Think their expression neverending
        when you ask for anything
        receive it
                and are conquered

Notice
        how sensation acquits the charge
                you are an ordinary canary
And how this intertwining's a portal
This weakness   a surprising strength

Beautiful
        because dear friends have turned to knowledge
And never-meant-much has no longevity

They will do well
They say they like it
        and say   like recovering communists
                that secrets may still be kept
                and so something of deprivation's put to use

A strange cargo for the duration
A longing to arrest that falling-to-pieces process
        one dance for all
        the feeling of inhabiting your body
                questioning why *this* body
                asking if that existence is the *only*

Learning "No!" as an answer

if another is part of your surrender

Chopin was chaperone to parterre
The entire theater filled
        and awaiting the art of dance
        the art of overthrown empire

Nothing in the night may prepare us
Your transformation
        is one time
                one chance
And your acceptance depends

What risk?
What atonement?
What satisfaction?

Believe and belong to the wilderness
Adam and Eve alive as long as the universe is young enough
You prosper with an ecstasy
        that is separate
        and not wishing to return to any routine connivance

Breathe in   breathe thorough every atom of the lagoon!
Be in love!

I will break down for once
Make it an emotional bottom
        the better to qualify
                for any adoration you may see fit

Dark ingenue   invention
What shall I call you?
And may you believe this lagoon is our own!
                        deep blue!

Every sense of yourself is strong affection
I will tell you every secret that was told to me
        when I wandered off-course as I could

Even Rock 'n' Roll was forgotten
And the stillness then   before
        prepares to receive *you*
        a *seeker* of truth

At the water's edge admonish
The Latin forest listens
        and guesses our intentions
Guesses tomorrow's at hand and traveling somewhere

Please!
There is something lost and it is final
                There is something irretrievable
one could not afford to lose track of
        and damage is all   destruction!
        you enter a wasteland!

How will it end?
An ancient palace is gone
        whole populations removed from their homelands
        some monstrous social engineering
The last kind glances before betrayal is enacted

There is a blankness   an empty place
And what is missing
        torments from elsewhere
                surrounded by art
Reads from a literature derived from life's last minutes
Art from ideas of outrage

If we fool around in the forest
        it will be a good going back to sleep
Like a natural development
All the fright that flesh can tell

While the salmon wait for a way out to sea
        lie down
        watch and imagine sea life's design
                and all its erotica

The cover of the Book of Love not giving anything away
        except things that happened a long time ago
                and are *topical* now

Your kisses combine
        to be a reconstructed *Tao*
Brand-new with non-meaning
                        from a mastermind

uncensored

Your kisses contend
        that overthrow is a simple garden done right
        with birds of your persuasion

Make yourself a widow with seduction
Since death comes one way or the other
        every time we are in concert

I almost didn't date you
                knowing how dangerous
                how unsentimental
                        may be a greater falling
                        and sudden

Have you killed me?
For once I was prepared
        for early Massachusetts, even
        the colony's inception
                        my *own* in 1943

I'm thinking you stole the key to Stone Lagoon
That you know its inventory truly
        naked   a way of life and collage

It was the surprise of *feng shui* refugia
Gravity's absence   that flying
                Stone Lagoon made moral

What time is telling
        and elegantly failing to fully translate

You have elicited the downfall of keepaway biology
And by this rescue
        continue to love words
                that have been returned to more basic noise

Say it was the science of lips
        and how that study increased intuition
Crawling around being mostly water
Remembered that flow
        and all the shapes its molecules make
                are a blank joy

black-basic-tragic

Ecstasy!
And spiritual *unseen* stars
        yet kidnap your being
And mothers and fathers are wanton lovers
Held mad!
        held to a torture
                to mystique and trepidation!

The day off that canceled the calendar's sand
No longer slippery
        and adhering to the glass

DRY LAGOON

It's not so dry just now

The rains have filled it in
Shallow ponds
             have displaced the pasture's memorial acres

So for awhile
       the lagoon is returned
               to yesteryear's freshness
               before the highway brings you by

Of Humboldt's lagoons
       this was exceptional
       this was the one that raised the most questions
If only a scientist would come with explanations!

Wait!
The park headquarters   there's always that
Some ranger is there
       who will simplify the solid Dry Lagoon!

Hey!   maybe never mind   it's useful dry
Though questions persists as to *why* it is
       they are questions barely formed
               and subject to spring's distraction

WHITE MOUNTAIN   2227 FEET

There was a White Mountain named
    for the color said to carry all the others
And it was possible to see The Pure Land's summit

And its companion peak called Summit Mountain
As though only *that* mountain mattered
    had a top to it   bordered with privacy
    on the straight line of coast road
            to Sixes
            to Denmark
                Langlois
                  and Laurel Grove

And White Mountain *suddenly* arises
While Floras to Floras goes
    thin consonant "Creek" to the vowel of "Lake"
      and Boice-Cope Campground

And the lake is like a certain lagoon I know of
KOA waiting upon the contemplation of natives

An omelette's made in Denmark   the town
    as Scandinavian dreams expand
    and widen their plots for breakfast
Starting long as the fingers of tarot
      to the empty airport near to Cape Blanco
        in duskish December

Realism walks with absent air traffic personnel
    who are gone away
      to inscrutable oblation
      to the faraway ferns of a southern canyon

There was a White Mountain once
In a movie seen so long ago the celluloid's lost
    and the light that lanterned the show
      in the snow of darkened theaters

The story concerned a team's struggle to prevail
In an otherwise vigorous and honest ascent
    of the movie's title   *The White Tower*

Another White Mountain it was
Blurry and blinding
        with impassible ice
                a towering *ultima thule*

At Calf Ranch Mountain the wind is gusting
Gusting Edson Butte as well
Both enveloped
        as if by a lucky concept
                that lets you escape from the predictable

The First Millennium's light upon us
Like fourteen hours of Times Square compressed

Elsewhere Dibble Glacier is suitably cold
        with the cold of Antarctica
                and come to the color that carries all the others

In absentia is Glenn Gould
He's gone south unseeing sans companion eyesight
The next thousand years
        to be a new lake made from the rain of reason

There's this thing called "Hell"
How can anyone stand it?
        even Stone Butte   stand it?!

A cypher must allay the suffering
A flame at the hem of Guardian America
        the statue paralyzed that was *already* stone

Dreamful gnosis
        White Mountain
                Year 2000 jebel!

At the end of a straight line
        drawn from the Sinai suddenly and westward

The town of Denmark is a country gone
Come away in search of Hamlet
        lost in formal meditation
                on bought-and-paid-for obloquy

The Pure Land is Round Top
        Grouslous
                and Eightmile Prairie
                its mountain

There was a White Mountain wintering with all the rest
In proximity to Denmark
        its predictable miles away

Offenbach's sopranos   at early evening
        will perform at Paradise Point
                their arias *also* resounding
                        among the safe summits of Antarctica

An iterum cypher

E.T.A. has a place to live   officially
He's jocular, even
        telling stories of heightened awareness
With Offenbach applying neroli to Antonia
        on her mountain of C Major rainbows

I'm a foal at the hillside spring
With a body language that says, "*Ecoute*!"

The least *ligia pallasii*
        skitters accordingly in the spray zone of Gull Rock
                and finds the crevice
                best suited
                        for music appreciation
Like a recess of the Paris Opera

The isopod works hard   *plays* hard   in Hell

Glenn Gould's banished fingers
                        like knotweed entwined
The theater of seaside is grandstanded, too
With Langlois   French-frilled

The bat star crouches somewhere
And bears a scientific name for the sin of scavenging

The rest of my life must be Russian sacrifice
For the crown of White

Summit
        Stone Butte   and
                Eightmile Prairie Mountain

Edson smothered by the blankets of natives
A compassion of already companions
A veneer of northern tribes
                their somehow kinky Viking colony

I'll have an aerial view of the White Cape
Knowing Fox Rock is a reef island further
        the Pure Land's last stop
        last step   to Asia
Fox Rock overrun with anthropods
                burrowing for privacy
                though they're creatures of the throne of the Pacific

And the audience-sea is a patient monarch
It waits upon the next mountain's ruin
        and all the spirits of erosion
                that spy the weak link in the bastion of high ground
                and are rolling Sixes in the presence of a Crystal

Glenn Gould is at peace

Though
        in the midst of the piano bar's crowd noise
        he's an uncertain statue
Playing braincase boogie of no time's timeout
A white noise Okietown antagonism
                dancing to the palmetto's flutter
                straight line concept

A movie of ferns and formal meditation at the foot of tarot

On faraway Telegraph Avenue   Berkeley
Where   foretold in the telling is:
        you would to *these* flowers come
        in time for their so erudite departure
                                for all-colors' candor!

There was a white light once
In the union of the forest   crested
A just-so summit

as though Hell had a ceiling
     that hinted of God's only lonely

A longevity such
    that the straight lines of airport slacken
       and a mountain's wear is sudden lowering
       and declining
         to a valley of pins-and-needles

Paris just a gossamer lisp
The annelid awakening to wonder

THREE STONES

Three stones
Three leftover crags by Stone Lagoon
Three improbable incisors
     positioned southside the barrier sand

The binoculars say, "Go!"
Find out their strength and geologic cunning
     there on the wide way north-south

Small-scale precinct
Reef at the juncture
     of mindset and sea-set   a prediction
Darkness has added these rocks to its caravan of hours

The next full moon is tonight
The spring flood's gallons and gallons
     have gone to sea through the soft, soft sand

Three stones a part of prophecies
     till *now* delayed
     by solitude's heretofore stopgap revery
Dollars and cents postponing their bleak ascendant preference

Have no doubt
     they do belong to conspiracy's faith in depth

Time was important while it served za-zen
Time *was*   *no* cost was too great
     to ensure a narcist agenda moved forward

Then these stelae made promises east and west
Said the lagoon should have a gate
     and the gate   three-part acknowledgement
A toll to be assessed   a deal made

We have captured an oceanographer
He's telling all he knows qualified by conceit
Between explanations he's duct-taped
     while we painstakingly *review* the lecture so far
     such we are thorough
        and not in any hurry

He goes on in fits and starts theorizing origin
Or he's urged to hurry along
        get to the good parts

He's given sandwiches
Is pledged financial assistance
        for the institute of higher learning he works for

The three little rocks are a provocative trinity
And reflection trends to *other* threes
        Father, Son and Holy

Masonic Mozart's E Flat triad
"Ready, set, *go*!"
The universe of bases and strikes

You begin a list like an outline
A list before you know your listing
        before self-consciousness ends it

Someone make me a job
        the pay to include surveillance of Stone Lagoon
I'll make a living as chronicler
                        what happens
                        the comings
                        goings

Thinking populations still conform
That it's still the Younger Dryas
        Ice Age scarcity

I would be open to delusion
                there's time and space enough
I would look at the lagoon carefully
        plot a rowboat's reconnaissance

In no time at all it's Japanese Nature!
The realm of rocks and banzai
There would be no invasion
        no body-snatching

The Empire of the Sun staying put in Asia

These hours   obey
    these hours of noesis
        saying what I couldn't say
        before the white sky's shell had cast its spell

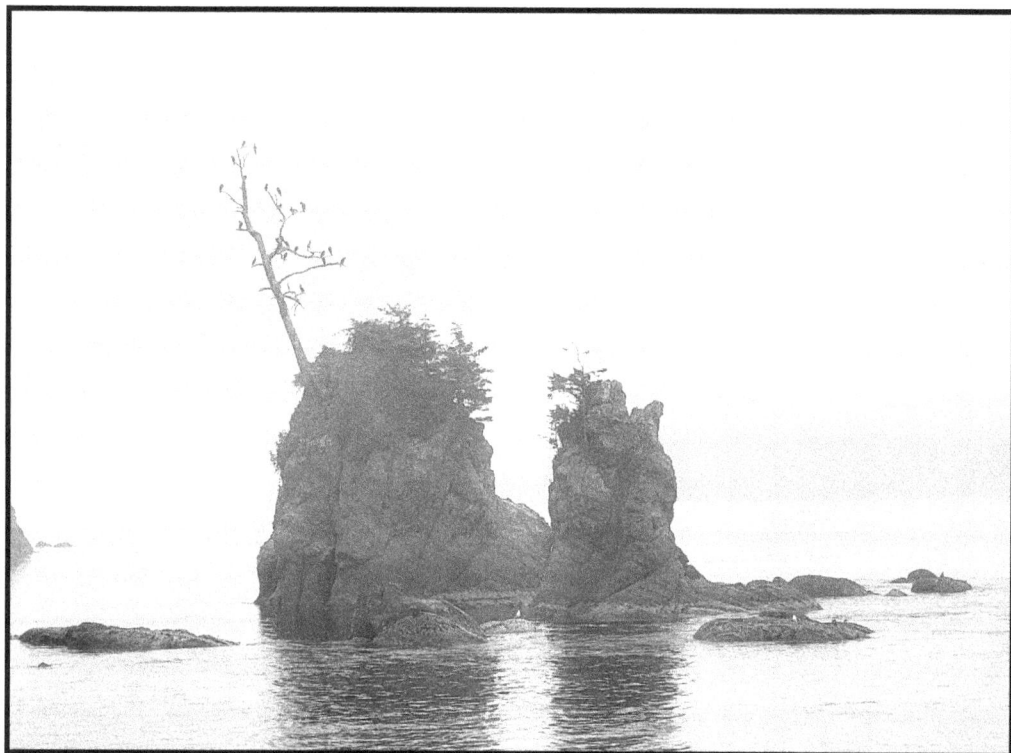

FRESHWATER LAGOON   PRISTINE

If I said it was pristine
      the opposite of picric
         am I then believing too much
         in a name
           Freshwater Lagoon?

Nothing too much encroaches
Though distant settlements there are
      the opposite *shore* seems inaccessible

The only lagoon with a highway on its bar
      a shame!
Nevermind the perfectly good *inland* route
Someone said to go straight across
          well   okay, I guess
          I'll love it anyway
There!   I'm *over* and accepting the straightaway

But where are the trailers?
            motor homes?
            campers?
They used to be parked and lined up
        what the highway was good for
What do you know about this?
What have you seen that wasn't whizzing by?
      and will you tell me?

Very well   I'll be still
     be the only one this day
        to stop by the oh-so-accessible sea
        to stop in all that vacancy of absent visitors

Not summer today
Yet consider the sea and all its edges
      like a prelude to knowledge
      summer notwithstanding

I will not continue
      and enter into anything like wisdom
Just lean a little forward
Catch wind of it

the information prior to understanding

The colors there are
        are clues to this learning
Even Paint-by-Numbers would do just fine
                high-speed internet left out of the exercise

Please tell her I wanted to bring her
Bring her all the way to Freshwater Lagoon
I am still keen she should see it as it is just now
        without the crush of tourists

Ah!   there you are!
There is much we might decide to do
And *Scrabble* in the wind
        without magnets
                would certainly be a challenge
Spelling the many lower case passwords
                        to Freshwater's domain

The absence of campers
        like a portent past the "peak of empire"
Somehow you know this
Somehow the downhill is apprehended

We could talk about it
        drinking whiskey in the dark   *you*, anyway

Where's your harmonica?
Get that harmonica going, clever girl!
Humboldt citizen   due backstage the park theater!

Your songs shall fill it with country western sensibility
And where's the end of it, once begun?
The pristine
        the free and wayward
                nothing!
                the echoes *attest* to this nothing!

Never mind we are history's stand-ins
Enacting Herodotus
        rewriting   righteous
        with much emotion

Please!
No longer wait
        no longer never mind the monsters
                in place of tourists

The two of us in time to enter a trance state
Informally   straightaway
The lately-departed
        still running their ghostly engines awhile

A memorial blankness
        forever after-imagining their former greatness

Close your eyes
        you see the stationary cavalcade
        while I hold you in my arms
The phrase like an aspiration
                derived from all we see of marine enchantments

Faraway is near   and belonging to a faith of miles
Look *there*!
        and with camera eyes imagine emulsion
                knowing realtime professes
                        you are precious reconstruction

Have you come prepared?
No matter
        for the landscape has plans
        voiceless commands
And hypnosis so subtle
                no trick of the will
                        may rise to the occasion of refusal

You were living on your own
Do not change
        you were born to do no one's bidding!
Pure escape become a *raison d'etre*

There are other languages than human!
Your ears are adorable!
Have I said so?
        and if I have   do you believe me?
        believe me *completely* or only in part
                hearing echoes of a desire to please?

There is nothing I would rather be doing
      than looking for you
And Freshwater Lagoon's as good a place to start as any

The canoes have come ashore   they never tipped
You and I are still afloat and search for comfort

Any book you wish to read together
      that one is *my* choice too
            it's the company that matters
Had you desired to read the Yellow Pages
      I should not have objected
                  though Follett's lying there
                  the inevitable novel
                        with intrigue to keep you happy

Just hearing your voice is enough of a plot
One last book
      before oblivion
      that gentle destruction you promised
            those violins you summoned
Here to eternity   here to a*nywhere*

Are you still here?
And do you know how many felonies
      how *many* I'd commit to keep you happy?

May your strange strings enlighten!
Create new personalities to save the world!
New friends never known
      who will defy history's demands
            and let you and I stay alive at Freshwater Lagoon

With perspectives never considered
With flame-blackened assumptions refused

Please allow it!
Like ancient poetry revived
      the first few lines
      that were not strictly chants to capricious deities
And before the impulse to archive
When "No!" was said nicely

Sometime reflect you are always yourself
Even starving
        in dispute or agreement

"Time well-kept"
        as Richard Hack had once informed
                with a perfect edge

This could be Sunday   the way the light is
Sunday   and cathedrals you built
        with tidy timber
                with*out* suspicions

Guilt has dried its tears
Simplified
        lost political value
Let's be face-to-face
                and confess Infinity awaits
                        the wind
                        ourselves

Those loud imprecations
Like lists of complaints
        "What do you *mean*, 'I exaggerate'?"

It doesn't matter
The absent recreational machines
        were a colony intent on bridgehead
                with beer and wine and weed and fishing

Take liberties
Be a creature of 6 Gallery
        at large on the north coast
        still tethered to cracked-open dharma
The Super Vacation   all expenses paid

Pushed past the point
        of reading glasses held with speculation
Enter strangers who shall commingle
Engines running

Were they raptured?
Both the heroes and villains
                embarrassed by selection?

Well, they are certainly gone
As we are
     to every dune
        and spurious sea grass tuft

FRESHWATER'S GATE

Rusted entry iron   no luck
Go around
        go to sea
                wondering what the gate could be
                        besides symbolic contrivance
                        an ochre-yellow warning
With a red diamond arresting development

Take a picture as reminder of its unexpected placement

With so much surrounding
                it's surprising any structure was attempted
Yet   in all the sprawl of the barrier bar
        the gate's presence seems an agreeable reference

A formal element
                included
                introduced
But when was its installation decided on?

Perhaps a committee
        on purpose
        proposing near and far
                with metal geometrical swinging
With *access* considered

Little gate
        like an honor system made a physical thing
                and not just talk over champagne

What earlier date is the gate?

Oh, do not drive down there!
You can't drive past it!
This is to separate!
the beach is conclusion
        and you can stay
        to see oxygenation's progress
                the colors
                a pleasant serendipity found
                                that is tactile

The uses the gate may have
          though left to salt spray
                    its accelerated decency
                    mutability's exemplary demo

Let's talk about it before we disintegrate ourselves
Before we are too upset about all this
And before the gate is weathered too much
          there'll be a photograph to prove what was taken away
          what matches identities

Yes, let the gate symbolize
          that   in spite of coastal access
                    there is not *true* access to its truer nature

You may write about it forever
Even in all of your lifetimes
          and not discover your heart's desire

THE OLD ROAD AROUND

There's a stillness east of Freshwater Lagoon
        like a derelict jungle
That old road around is now *secondary* travel

An enclave's elevated acres there
        are the only exception
        to unwrapt and unspoiled

That which could take a visitor's attention
        so that a book is closed
                for the sake of origins and emptiness
The collapsible day prepared to be empathic

That old road around
        imagined as something for a later After All
That is *new* and carefully inspected
What is burnished set aside for softer lighting

So you leave off dense fellowship
                to see a thinning population
                embracing former soldiers

The extra twistings the old road afforded
        were squiggles better known then
A sinuous slowing and enhancement
The curves subtracted that were necessary highway
        now the unused meanders

If you care for not *every* woman
Just your wife
        and can think of no one else for once
                then Freshwater Lagoon is full of purpose

The sense of an earlier *altruistic* leaning
Some secret flyby
        and science fiction of fins and blastoffs
        in craft so flimsy the cardboard was showing

It is a metabolic wonder
        that the crew persists
                and rescue's effected

In the starveling day be chosen sponsor
With Freshwater's mainstream telling things that you know
         and know not
Open wide to a med school
         that everywhere holds its Everywhere
                  and thrives on hypochondria

Across the water
         the clearing invites a colony of one scholar at a time
It *could* be an outpost of Harvard
And the research
         whatever it is
                  to take some time

It's 101's *former* life
         that takes a little more patience
You make it around and winding
The contour to be verbified
         and made powerfully descriptive

Let's walk it like a trail now!
A very *good* trail
A way of slow-motioning the auto ride
         so that you don't miss a thing

Even sleepwalking   you're aware
And prescind the highway's ghostly engineering
         in perspective
Staying tuned to a radio
         if it has the AM or FM needed
                  to clear the coast range

Are you coming back for more
         finally sure
         the lagoon is sufficient recreation?

Cell phone tossed you blend in
Seeing the same thing
         that once in Massachusetts you saw
                  that seemed impossibly far away
                  yet you lived there anyway
Not minding how the color blue would haze the vision

You want to watch the ripples
    to see their glitter-fickle facile persuasions
    like a sense of finance mostly fractal in nature
And that lends itself to life after the death of the dollar

A medium   watery
Wherein the fish are explainable deductory beings

Behold Manhattan!
Greenly do this
The State of New York, even
                prior to Contact
The mood of a metropolis nowhere detectable
    its raucous garbage trucks
        sirens and impatient taxicabs

Everyone has a breaking point
And so outreach
    their agony complimentary
        a very good devil's work

To be *savored*
If you're that demon
    that sits
    and waits on its haunches
          for leftovers

I'll ask you one more time what was asked before:
Will you just go
    and kill me at the portal you represent?
Right there   the best of your best spells to complete?

That super-soul of myself you've made
    may take every part of me
    and my otherwise amazingly imperfect being
      and lend surprising judgment in departure!

Only fulfillment on the scale of Greek pantheon union
    may chance to touch it off
When suddenly   because of your caresses
      everything comes to an end
      because what could follow
        that would not be a letdown?

An old road around made quite modern
Its quaint country route turned thoroughfare
     without so much as one pothole repaired

I understand that language connects us all, all right
You must appear
     right here   right now
          on Freshwater Lagoon's bar
          to interpret such dreams
               as we have had occasion to dream

Then the text
     that has started so modestly here
          must increase
          to include *some* version of your visit
               that may be virtual

Before the brain shuts down from too much solitaire
A game   paradoxically
     that is best played in crowds
     and from the earliest ages, too
               in worst case scenarios

These are the inclinations known
While stopped and staring at woods to the east
     that were so many greens and yellows
          new crayons were needed
          and one is startled into purchase

Thinking as well
     that those cauliflower crowns of the forest
     there   beyond the lagoon
          would help *anybody* learn the names of Hindu gods!

CAPE SEBASTIAN

"Squall"   the word with the "q"
The high-scoring *Scrabble* word
  applied late in the day
  to the immense and distant curtain coming down
Due west of Sebastian's summit

The coastal trail a tunnel of love in the flora
Limbs and leaves
  all the brambly slopes
    tear-dropped and gleaming

And the shower that was out to sea
  came a little closer
  broadened
    its cloud gone and smeary
Perfectly enhancing the nineteenth hour
    of a desperate Tuesday

When only the bulwark of Sebastian offered solace
The squall intensifying
  like a neutral philosophy
    forced to find its way to a conclusion
The sea a slate accomplice

Transaction's example
Thought made visible
  a complementary sky and sea
  come together as Screen Gem perfection
A gray serendipity's sunset

The show   unattended theater   except for the playwright
.

PORT ORFORD'S UNEXPECTED PIANO

Paula's Bistro after many rainy miles
And looking carefully for deer in the night
Noting The Sisters three
    and how their bulk was a darker dark

And after that unmistakable trio
    past Ophir
        Euchre Creek
            and the loopy tilting asphalt
              the lights   of the Bistro!

Thought to go in there and see a map
See a way east that wasn't *guessing* east to La Pine

But   on entering
    there was a Baldwin black
    a Baldwin piano black
With red, blue and pink candles upon it

I'd found the *perfect* road trip piano!
It looked playable
But I'd play it playable or not if allowed
    for it was too good to be true
        a glorified plaything
        early evening

Many generals have paused their plans
    hearing Chopin after dark
When battle was then impossible
Being dissuaded from any military goals

While the rain poured down
    I asked Paula if it would be okay
    could I play
        go to college again
        pet the cats in the backyard
           review an earlier existence

Bring it all up to date in the dark of Port Orford
The unexpected piano
    placed in the wind and the rain

The only instrument of Mozart
        all day and night of traveling
          thoughtfully tuned to the key of construction

The mind made floor-by-floor

"Will you allow it, Paula?
On a run up the coast to Bandon?
I would be so grateful to you
     a minimum repertoire to go with the outside storm?

"I am beautifully stranded here
And at your service
      with a C Major sonata from the eighteenth century
All sickness to dispel

"A sonata for the cedars atop the Port Orford Heads
      and what is still unknown over there
Music for the unseen Battle Rock Wayside
The absence of handguns drawn
For the surf that has never looked so left behind
     this beautiful Tuesday"

Main Street's the highway   101 the number

And Paula spoke:
"Yes, please!
You are my *guest*   feel at home!"

And I made the best homemaker I could
     the black piano coaxed and accepting
        Mozart and more

Paula wanted to know what music was played
Her husband had named the bistro after his wife
And   getting to know them
     I thought I could live there
     even if they were the only friends made
For they were sufficient grace and acquaintance

Moving to Port Orford?   an easy thing to do
Save La Pine for when Burning Man calls
Make a big city out of a small one

An adagio progressed
        while two tables of patrons lingered
                their after dinner drinks sipped thoughtfully

I wanted new shoes for those pedals' possibilities
                    shading soft to loud
                    piano to *forte*

Wanted a makeover based on adoption
I'd be a regular
        and nights the hurricanes come
        they'll come to the Bistro
                silently grateful for what the Baldwin can tell

Its multicolored candles all in a row
                        and lighting one by one

FOG AT THE SUMMIT

Altitude's involved
1485 feet
     to get over
         and down
            with *caution*

Fog like a ghost
Green and gray up there
     green when it's faint and *dimly* green
     green the way it's grayed out with cloud stuff

You may say it's one addiction for another
But the fog world encountered in crossing to the Klamath
     was a distance worthy of further study

When obfuscation's a color scheme
     to go with the noun
         the slant of the crest
         like a seven percent aspiration

They destroyed the woods
     to make a passage worthy of to-and-fro
           north and south
           going on and going over

Who would have ever guessed the chess of that engineering?
Its everywhere winding
       exactly conceived
          a road to nothingness

Fog so thorough one yawns
Pulls over
     to enjoy a first magnitude mist
     and misty *soporific* stratocumulus

Descend to the Klamath
And know its watershed's miles go on and on
     connector miles
In a morning fog
       that will enter afternoon
       before a meridian knows better

the sun overslipped

It seems the engine's noise is muffled too
And dampened machinery
        takes the first imperceptible steps to rust
        its polish and protective wax notwithstanding

Real-time befuddlement commences
Trying to understand
        or identify
                the object of your desire

Talk about it!
No one knows the day or hour
                                a May 21st?
                                good as *any* day to die
Good day
        still a tosspot confused
                anything might as well go
                rhyme and reason included

It's good to be enshrouded
Good clouds to go with the moods of a junior priest
        unsure of his profession
Blessed is he who acknowledges uncertainty

A fogbow beginning
        the rapture must include me
I for one am staying   right here
                        part of a cautionary tale

Fog of the crystal beginning to clear
Or some argument that increased confusion
You were trying *so* hard to make sense, too!
We both were talking at the same time
        the argument a bickering
                and diffusion of energy

You'll catch your cold in the damp
        thousands of dollars of damp
        in the heights
                between Orick
                and the Hoopa Valley Indian res
                        where Lost Man Creek tumbles down

And   lost in that fog
        still you search for a way to Fern Canyon
        and Gold Bluffs
                the place you pronounce
                        with a great desire to be there!

The pass like a question:
"When do you notice 'down' either way?"
        the arch of the summit so gradual a curve
                the question goes unanswered

You find you look forward
To the elk that wander on the prairie to come
Remembering
        how a cat once rolled in their presence

It was the large and small   both oblivious!
And   comically   the setting
        a house and yard and garage
                should they *charge*, those elk…
If they aggress
        I guess
                the cat knows it's a "no go"
                and undeserving rough treatment

Unfair to hurt
In fact, she was protected
        elk as bodyguards
                could use one myself
One who would just take charge of the wheel awhile!

The temptation for side trips then averted
No Davison Road driven down to the sea
No Bald Hills Road the *other* way

Although the weather's a nebula's metaphor of vagueness
        yet hating and killing are held in abeyance
Confusion has a purpose
Persuading a truce be established
                between ought and should

The fog is waiting
        in a thrall of water droplets

to consider it may be best
for a creature of timeout
Somewhere after Orick
But before the casinos that lurk on the Klamath
past Starwein Flat
and all that winding way

As much as I'd *like* to
Alder Camp will be saved for certain summer weather
It is the principle of fog that matters most
There's something wrong
that only the contemplation of gray will make right

Therefore dedicate the ride to that
A great project
made of next to nothing at all
what clouds are   and thankfully

The opposite of guns
Though its dun gray mimics the metal

The fog at the summit *invited*
A *kidnapping* fog
that would prepare a place for you
in its fog castle   a guest room
Captivity to include the windblown evergreens

You'd go to bed early
just to fall asleep to their branches
their white noise raging!

Perhaps an aerie
safe from the fate
of a creature that lives in a puppet mararite
whose body whorls
and slanted axial threads
are not miracles enough
to deter the dire whelk
or the ravages of the nudibranch

Safe for now
For you know
another go 'round could put you in a shell

All the more urgent
    there be a version of Now
        as near as sylvan moisture may allow

WILSON CREEK'S SEA LEVEL ENDING

Where it empties
Where once I went
    to see a great cleft
    a giant rock that broke

Where James and I
    made a serious study of the sea
    enjoying the place
        as a prelude to a great understanding

Lines on a map   connecting
Wilson's cold stones beneath the bridge
Last stop
    before the swerves to Crescent City
    when you're raised
        then lowered
        to the tsunami hazard zone

Thinking of Japan
And how a long way off
    can transmit chaos in   chaos out
      all day
      until equilibrium's achieved

Quake like a rock
You can see its halves had a history
    the whole of it sundered
        some hour of unendurable weakness

The split an uneven alley
The ocean's sound acoustic
    while you walk it   touching walls
    a place of crosswords' ancient ricochet
      a *preachy* echo   remorseless as Space

Its frantic spilling   everywhere

Each semi-dome a seeming pluton
An orphan of Yosemite
    though its dark complexion suggests otherwise
      oh, try to remember the geology!

"Big-granite-rock-that-broke!"
Said as if it were a long Indian name

And I tried
        with repetitions
                to reduce it to nonsense syllables
                needing translation

Said it *fast*   many times
In bouldering
        hopping
                clambering

Said it to the kelp and seaweed gardens
Said it to barnacles
        barely visible
        in the splash-zone's upper limits
                        where they somehow adhere

Said it like a *nudnik* intent on extreme annoyance
        till the phrase comprised hamartia!

But since I was solo the second time
        no one was upbraided
                nor was silence attempted
And I was free to plink
Free to vocally target the birds and seals

Wilson Creek the excuse for escapade
        trippingly performed
                        the beach like a showroom!

WILSON CREEK   THE HOUSE

The large house   back from the shore
        painted green on the upper floor
        tan on the lower
A two-toned extravaganza
                its gables slanting extravagant retreat

Five families could thrive
Generation to generation there
                while the creek well-watered them
Call it a resort of one mansion
        hugely recreational
        Nothing's heyday

And Rachmaninoff's relatives
        wait for visitors and Orthodox priests
The attic's full of keepsakes
The science of borscht a study in red

New works commissioned nightly
The spirit of Tchaikovsky hovers there
        amidst conversations' fugues
                and the everlasting babble of children in pajamas
                preparing for a damp coastal night

The boulders of the shore
Like grave stones   upturned   upended

But the house's light green
        is a permutation of the Summer Palace
        waiting on a virtual dynasty
Tan is the steppe
                the color of Cossack dreams
                where violence keeps its idolators

Oh, the house is of *interest*!
Very great interest
This coast might well have ended up Russian

Let the enclave at Wilson Creek be outpost
        "Seward's Folly" revisited
Perhaps that land bridge will appear in the north

And Beringia once more join the Old World and the New

Then may you walk   in an arc
        from the shores of the River Lena
        to Wilson Creek
                and beyond that to Fort Ross south

It's just a Russian house
A dacha
        and this is not the place to analyze empires
But this *is* the place
                where a green and tan house
                        was built outside of history

We've made it a Russian doll house
And peopled it with favorite composers
We've assigned it a *century* too
        century of dresses
                blowing in Sinatra's summer wind's perfection

Lucky estate
And all fleeting privilege possible!

KLAMATH RIVER CASINO

The Hoopa ghosts go away   but they go on
A casino is left
        the map's pink patches joined
                to make a river's reservation

So carefully drawn
        the longitude and latitude
                are incremental
                keeping a width either side of the river

The boundaries
        east-west and north-south
                conform to the Four Directions
Enough sun to make it interesting

The grass will grow
And every tree stretch out
        in those delineated squares
        as needed

There's a casino that says "It's ours!"
The land's geometry's sold and shaded pink
Proceeds to benefit the tribe
                        and all its children

The white man's tantara
        that frightened the birds every day
        that is *still* too noisy
                and willing acquisition all over

But someday gamble there
A humble pioneer
        with no further westward to go
                increasing the odds of winning that way

Though everything is not religion
        you must chant to improve your chances
Rob the casino if possible
Be supernaturally skillful
        the only one with such a weapon!

Those overlapping squares insure the river's set aside
A GPS will tell you
      if you're in   or out   of Hoopa jurisdiction

The river floods
Spring has intensified
A life savings flowed into the chips of the casino
A lot can happen
      this day like a home stretch

I'm wearing a feather
Filling in for full-fledged native
Cards?
     keno?
          craps and roulette?

Enter into pink's restriction   The Zone
As easy as cruise control engaged
     the reservation perforated a hundred ways
Its airspace overflown
         with jets
         satellites
         and meteors

There will be sports in the casino   game results
The trick is to intuit
     the way a hunter knows
        the prey's close by
        will be overwhelmed with premonition

I'm scared to death of losing
A game
    a sister
And that fear must other ways travel
       and somehow be made a useful stressor
       an important part of the story of survival

You gamble in Hoopa Valley
Near Hunter Creek's entry into the Klamath
     just before the ocean's honor of truthful information

Put the money you risk in your left pocket
Your winnings in the right
     and when the risk pocket's empty

you're *done*!

Just drive 169 to Klamath Glen and get acquainted
Lo!   and behold!
     history's rewritten
     as a brand new book of good questions
Remember this!   never forget!

The ghosts are looking for another chance at life
Like a human experiment
              installing intellect

The valley has more to reveal
Be a witness with a lucky streak
     and stay until the Indians say, "Enough!"
     until your hair falls out
     until money has no meaning
        until a higher authority than God gives you a pass

And *please*   one minute at a time!
Your games of chance are better played
     the Klamath to be uncensored
        and their river made a magical bath of miles

We'll have a look at Flint Rock later
        in an increasingly dangerous world
But I can tell you right now
     the world is   *hourly*   preparing
        to be the paradise demanded by all the slackers

Only thing is
     there's no provision for room and board

I want to say
       the casino will
      in time
         accomplish its purpose
        to help the helpless
          and excuse the inexcusable

Please contact the chief
     if he's still around
     if he hasn't moved on

Oh, there was a "Chief Wahoo" once
In a childhood north
In the tan clay
      my sister and I would play
      with small figurines
         one of which acquired a name
On our knees and cruising the sandpit
    to make a story all afternoon
    starring "Chief Wahoo"

In a sense we were independently wealthy
As children are apt to be
    in all the outdoor compartments of the day
The way a *century* can be crammed
      in only a few of those twenty-four hours!

In daydreams were the plots conceived
With love were they assigned tiny statues
    like talismans   Indians for sure
    our own western close to a timeline
      so that we led double lives
Past supper, even

I say that Wahoo lives right here in the Hoopa
Respected leader
Let him know
    I've come to reprise a distant Renton
    same playground
      in Washington
        the State that's not the District

Childhood damaged by new homes
The clay covered up
    as ancestral lands were built upon

We're wanting sticks and stones
The uses of flint
Wanting to answer back the birds
    on a paseo by the river
      the deep and rapid river of the spring

Then enter the casino with supernatural powers
In fact, *run* the casino   perfectly assured
The dice just jumping of their own accord

Roulette revolving a *comprehensive* plan
　　to make you rich
　　if you will only write the right lyrics to go with good fortune

Like a shaman   exert the power
　　that gambling's accoutrements obey
　　that the slots will follow
　　　　to let their oranges and lemons align
　　that every chip placed is sure to be an opportunistic chip
　　　　　as if its career
　　　　　were bound   mysteriously
　　　　　　to yours
　　　　　　to a hunch
Everything ratcheting unlikely!

A *usable* frame of mind
The same as a spell
　　and nothing but psychic

The house is at a loss
　　to explain a spike in the take
As if all things were arriving perilune
Brand new
　　when you totally forget the words
　　when the words are making infamous what was so common

Feeling lucky in the aisles
Going as a sleepwalker to some reward
　　with the butterflies of waiting for a friend to show
　　like all the hours a stage contains

A stasis   stoppage
Suspended belief, all right

Gambling's a baby
The "third condition"
　　the winnings beyond just man and wife

The child like superstition *itself*
　　that says
　　　　as Jimmy said to the Hotel Utah in San Francisco:

"You can call me 'Baby'
　　　　and all night and day

"You can call me 'Baby'
                    never forget!"

CAMP KLAMATH

Almost any ailment there's a remedy
Albeit the cure can stay unknown

We thought about that
      camped near the Camp called Klamath
      with all of that river moving
            in the darkness beyond the fire's embers
And there was still *enough* fire to strobe the forest
      its orange facade unsteady nighttime scenery

Medicine was the topic in the near blackout
How the word "medicine" *itself* was almost healing
      and made us imagine the plants
          all the herbs
          and roots
              their forgotten uses

Even the chiefs have lost track
Talking of the shaman too
      and whether magic is possible in a land of cars

Still   no one was sad   no
The discussion was good
      and someone had taken the trouble
          to put hot-and-sour soup in a thermos
Kept it a secret till the fire died down!

Surprised and pleased we drank it down
And thanked China, too
      grateful for what was in the thermos
      but also for *big* things that had *not* happened to us

Like toothaches in the wilderness
And sprained ankles
      and foreclosures
          and speeding tickets

Klamath was a destination
Far enough and no further
      to be temporary dwellers
          in the watershed's miles

    in the mostly cloudy sunset
There was not a clue the sky would clear
            and show its stars after all

It was to be almost a desert's clarity
And the stars abnormally glittered
    their colors somehow exaggerated twinkling

So that it seemed the sky was a technicolor atlas
A Hubble view without that instrument's aid
And we were silent with x-ray vision
    seeing more
        more than we had ever known in looking up

There was no explanation for what we saw
And the strangeness increased
    as   at first
        at the horizon
        then filling in the rest of the sky
            connecting lines began!

Making constellations familiar and *un*familiar
    golden
        silver
        and flickering like the stars themselves

Until   gloriously
    the outlines of animals
        birds and dippers
          were complete
          and they sparkled intensely!

And the squares
    triangles
        and other geometry
          dazzled too
          adding extra starshine
          to what was already a fascinating clarity!

To say it was a rare sight
    ignored the fact it was *impossible* what we saw
But whatever the phenomenon
    we shared its uncanny physics
And were prepared for any miracle the sky proposed

An intuition began   an instinct
Like a research of seven seconds
A doctorate that flashed
            and flamed its thesis
            simulcast the instant the star book appeared

Like a child's astronomy primer
                  its golden threads joined
         and made celestial a tribal mythology
         as if this was the way the universe matured

With tracery to confound us in our forest hideout
            lost as we wanted to be
            but *careful*-lost

And other voices
         began to soothe the demons of this world
As one-by-one they were given homes up there
         given some perspective
            the same dreams as angels'

Allowing them to reprise an innocence
Their deep-down choice as wannabe spirits
Who just needed a lifting up   some elevation

The glowing geodesic almost informal
Lines which
         while each was the shortest distance
            still seemed drapery

Try not to cry?
No!   cry for good reason
      maybe a reason like:
            it appears the deep down subconscious
                  has come
                  like a kingdom
                     to the Klamath
And its psyche's beheld that was kept in a shell
      that magically cracked!

Or   we couldn't keep a lid on love's imaginings
Just one sorcerer walking at the fringes of the forest
      where our embers

pulse their pale orange coals in the day's coda

Confessional hearth
    that made the night a living room
        of gaping children
        children of the Hoopa Valley's sustenance

A remedy for what we had

EUREKA

i.   "Since 1943"

At Washington Street
    and highway 101 called Broadway too
Just where Commercial
        the one-way   angles away
                it was still 1943!

It was still my birthday year
And a sign that said plainly "since 1943"

It was Mike's Drive-Up   The Hamburger King

Also serving chiliburgers
        original garlic fries
        long dogs
          and old-fashioned shakes

In the middle of a war someone said,
"Let's start a business
        and *stay* in business if we can!"

Good, Mike!   you've done well
Still in business?
    well, it *says* so
    but it's still too early in the day to say

The nearby Heritage Motel seems aptly named
If the burger joint's open
    well, it *seems* to be…
        there's somebody there
        what's he doing?

Oh, there's another business in the very same building!
The Shenandoah Film Production Studios
Hey, let's make a movie of everything
    a movie of Eureka
    a movie of Mike's drive-up
        and his first day up and running!

His enterprise bursting into life and delivery

Perhaps even
    the first Thursday of my life
        on another coast
            in a Massachusetts hospital

Wondering why in the world I should be in *this* body
    at *this* time
Born to see the first trip to another planet

Perhaps the first old-fashioned shake
    coincided with other firsts
           first step
           first word
           first tricycle ride

It *does* say "since 1943" and so am I
Here, give me the movie camera
It will be a whole production
    and every day we'll confer
        at 633 Commercial

An indie with a vision
        two coasts
        two businesses
One being variations on the theme of burger
The other a one-note sonata concerning why this when

Our film will be a double feature of wants and needs
We'll name names
    and say who went to war
    who stayed in Eureka

And eastward
    who bounced the baby
    and sang him safety songs

"Never skate where the ice is thin
Thin ice will crack and you'll fall right in
And come up with icicles under your chin
    if you skate where the ice is thin!"

The long street like a long hike
Part boulevard   part highway
    remembering the Pequot Beverage Company

that supported a family of five

Dad's gig
Mom's telephone company job came later
The other coast appreciate
     realize   here in Eureka in the morning

Consult the videographer
         best angle
         lighting
Recognize the sea is part of both scenarios
And heavy storms

101 the arterial
The palindrome highway
    like a manipulation done to a New England road
Altogether it's still too early in the day
    the garlic fries would go nicely with the neology I long for

The phrase
    that may set in motion appreciation
        of Mike's Drive-up and much more
That may complement the wondering
Which car first drove up

I'm thinking it had to be a Studebaker
A 1938 one   maroon perhaps
    with baseball on the radio
Everything local
      the town of Falk with lots of folks
      living creekside in a redwood valley

Redirect time's flimsy arrow
We're all due backstage
    for a production of alibis
    knowing not   and when
The last lazy sun sent midbrain
      and received in peace

Is this the dual life left behind?
A pinhole made
    in an experiential balloon
      that was too much expanding a churchly gestalt
      so that the choirboy's lost?

Yes   lost to chance and circumstance
Make a movie now
Keep it running
        and reify others' histories
        since 1943

A family's enterprise to know
Where Commerce starts branching from Broadway
Still an early grill
        in sight of malls and all their chains

Don't let go!   not here   not yet
Perhaps in caring for strangers
        one may get some good practice
                in time to be a hero to familiars

Eureka's been kind
Always beginning
        always starting out
                the introductory town
                town just visited
And an interest taken
                that would be strange in your homeland

Please tell me more, Eureka!
Your effortless seaside miles
What hypnosis that has happened
        to make Mike's Drive-up since 1943
                a liberty that must be taken

Believe and belong
                to this coast
                to mutism
                to witness
To average solitude
        entwined with communal sentiments

From the marina go
Past jetty north and jetty south
        go thoroughly out to sea
                a little sorry you hadn't thought to do so before

And wild out there   beyond the breakers

be a creature of the Humboldt Current till you die
daring to luff
      in the total gales that approach

Eureka is that sailing as much as Mike's
The entirety a tapestry
    pored over as writing is
        the collected letters found
        since 1943

Which   though downbeat-sad
    still elicit a well-mannered comedy
        coming close to perfection

And I'll not mind no piano's to be found
A hasty reconnaissance is all that's possible
That church or restaurant
    waits with a keyboard somewhere
Just so it's sufficient
        there's a sign
        a menu

A heritage to stay in day and night
Mending for the briefest of sartoris

Maybe the old-fashioned shake and not the fries
Since arriving Eureka
    there's only sweetness and light
    and eschewing tragedy's sobriety for once in your life

ii.   Denny's at 5th and C

At 5th and C
    in the seaworthy morning
        the friendly Denny's ladies had a lot to say

One said she'd come from the *other* Bay
"There are two Bay Areas
    and the smaller one's the best!"

Her daughter was a student at Humboldt State
Yes, the one on Thompkins Hill Road
That *very*

the rural frontage that was so foggy-cold that time
Frosty, even   you shivered!

Her daughter'd enrolled
And *so* did she enroll in Eureka's environs
        such a sensible outcome of college
        she was sure it was the best idea she'd ever had

Both women working hard at Denny's

The other waitress said to go to the music store
"It's just down the way"
She described a piano she'd bought and completely restored
Removing the paint so that the rosewood gleamed

If only I'd hypnotized her
        because I was under her spell
                and would *visit* the store right away
I was too much a stranger and not enough relative

For a brief moment we enjoyed a very loose association
We three
        two busy waitresses
        and an idle out-of-towner
                in conversation so interrupted
                the whole affair did fragment

And was lost to Denny's white noise
        with diabetic patrons anxious to pay

iii.   The Music Store

It was there, all right

A music store on 2 Street called
        not Second
It seemed a nice touch
Naked 2 without the "n" and "d"

It didn't have a piano
        and just a keyboard stood

Never mind

It *did* have something better than keys
A tabby cat all orange
        and waiting at the entrance for customers to come

And first thing it starts in purring
A very *loud* purring
        throaty and thorough
So that there's a pause
The man behind the counter
        allowing time for that feline intro to charm

The *formality*
        that must precede any questions and answers

Amidst many musical things
Songbooks
        saxophones
                clarinets and all their mouthpieces
                        cymbals and drums
                        guitars and accessories
The accessory *cat*
And the loud music of its purr!

Thank God for this tabby!
        the dander notwithstanding
The owner's a genius who speaks to cat lovers
He knows the sale's a distant second
        and such as myself will linger
                enthralled and captured
                more quickly than by a sales pitch

For the cat puts brakes to any haste
And hearing him purr makes a customer take time
All the time there is
        to find the instrument that will make that sound

We talked   the guy and I
        "Would a keyboard do?"
        "Kinda sorta"
        "You travelin'?"
        "More or less"
        "You like the cat?"
        "Yep!"
        "Well, look around"

"I will"

The tabby drooled and rolled

"It's 9 a.m.
The cat is so alive!
When do you close?
        and why *would* you close?
Oh, never mind that last   just be 24/7"

"Very funny!"
"Very adorable!"

The guy named the cat
        but I'd have to go back and be told again
                in order to tell you
Was it "Pearl?"

Piano cat
No mere keyboard would do
        but the cat would suffice
Play the *cat*
                its soft pedal and damper, too

Note the touch with satisfaction
The action easy
        a bit of Gieseking's Baldwin
                a colored Steinway kitty

Aw!   the baby fussy-bye is drooling
And sentimental
        that's good
        the cat truly cares
                and animates the state of poverty

Maurice Ravel would approve
He imagines a tabby lends support
        and suggests improvements
        that the score
                may then be a licked-clean inspiration

Another one of those situations
        where you really need a cat to make a go of it

The purring competes with a child's clarinet
The lesson in progress   barely tentative
        but the boy will live long and prosper
How you come back to basics
                    study the beginner
                    play with the cat
                        the lesson goes better after that

The cat can jump up
        to walk the keys that random chooses
            like accidental pedagogy
As if to say,
"Hey, kid   it's mostly listening   now listen to this!"

And he plinks and plunks contented instruction

iv.   Waking

Waking
        in the reasonable warmth of the Eureka motel
        the overpriced one
And thinking the lamp that was left on
                    was not artificial light
                    but a streaming sun

Thinking after the rain   mid-morning
        it was the class G2 star in a blue day's alphabet

Alarm light
And silent as the ghosts of this Oregon littoral
        unrestricted to the dark

Those spirits that lend obedience to exceptional desires
        thoroughly pre-dawn

v.   "Belinda's!, Belinda's!"

The waitress said,
        "Belinda's!   Belinda's!
        Bail Bonds   go there!"
And since I *only* go by recommendations
        I went

in the good faith that is always elusive

Walked to Belinda's from Stanton's
     where a waitress had noticed my listlessness in ordering

"Sir, are you all right?"
"Oh, yes!   sorry make it a scramble
     some onions
     chives
        a bloody Mary, I *mean* tomato juice"
"Sure coffee?"
"Uh, yeah, I guess"
"Anything wrong?"
"My son   a meth lab   he's been jailed
     it's awful!"
"I am so sorry to hear that!
     can you get him out on bail?"
"I don't know   I'm so stressed"

"Well, there's Belinda's near to L Street
When my cousin was busted
     for digging clams for the umpteenth
        we had occasion to use her services!"

I thanked her and said
     "That's some appetite for shellfish!"
        and continued to ruminate

Would a habit of my own
     have kept me apprised of my son's activities?
And   thus informed
     could I have somehow saved him?

Now in rainy Eureka he's pled not guilty
Well, that much is true
     the absurdity notwithstanding

Yeah, yeah   divorce!
And you never know all it may separate
An unfaithful wife
     but a son who loved her
     and wished her back in spite of everything done
        and everything said for the sake of propriety

And such unsentimental words at that

At Stanton's "since 1963"
      I considered how to go forwards
            that was not a backwards path

"Belinda!   please say what I do not know
I'll attend your recital
      and save my son if *you* can"

vi.   **When You Only Longed for Arcata**

Eureka
      when you only longed to go to Arcata
But Eureka was delayed too
      crossing to Samoa on three bridges

What did you see to do?
What did you imagine you'd find
            besides the islands themselves?

Having a long conversation with emptiness
Many generations will study the sea and its atrocities
The surgeon prays for her own recovery

Please, you must hurry!
Eureka will not provide
      its strange acres like a retro torment
      like turning a music book's pages
                  to get to unplayable

Regrets
And this wet weather knows
      rendezvous and tragic placement
Believe it and belong to your ending and tally of strangeness

But it's the opposite of a dangerous neighborhood

One might compare but it's just extra air

The *Marina's* free of crime
Smoke a joint to make it different
      make it right

        have some tofu
        you'll feel better after

The bridges are a free ride taken
There is steady rain for your rollercoaster
There are blue buildings in the downpour

Be in Samoa waiting on the Cookhouse to open
This is my foreign country to wander
      and 255 to drive
It doesn't matter it's Arcata you'll come to
           looping around

The Old Navy Base Road
And Humboldt like a sort of *super* lagoon
     and prelude to the rest up north
         Big Lagoon
         Dry Lagoon
         Stone Lagoon

Two islands   three bridges undulant
A downsized San Francisco Bay
     ever ready to hear your complaints

I wish my friend, James Cagney, Jr., were here

If he *were* he'd be here *again* because he was here *before*

I'd wanted to show him the jetty
     North Jetty   and did
        on the occasion of our tour
His favorite beach was Bandon in Oregon
Good work was done
He'd discovered a creek with his toes
     and the magic continued well past departure

Yeah, I wished I'd brought him
     for this is too much of Alone for proper note-taking
     like a surgery gone bad
        and you're gone to bed with recovery

Or the first elected president of a country
Having the task of changing the way things are done

in a place that had only known tyranny

I belong to no one after all
Is that clear thinking?
        or just more of the same miraculous sorrow?

Call someone at least
                tell them of that little-known highway
It should be better known for sure
Say you thought you heard a symphony playing
        without having slipped a CD into the slot

That it was the opening thirds of Brahms's fourth
The best E Minor the nineteenth century ever knew

This is the day of the groundhog
                            largely unknown
And no amount of February the 2nd celebrity
        is truly compensatory

"Hurry!"   hey, the word so very recently heard
"Be quick"
        and whispery as that symphony's urgings
There's no more money in the bank of emotion
                and there's a price on your head

I turned left
        on one of those lettered streets
        that happens to be a highway to take
Eureka   an alphabet town dying to spell
Its one-way streets a primer
        with pretty pictures of soul on its walls

How much gas?
The rental seems unsure   no matter
        there's leeway
                unknown but enough
                to cross over
And there's such a *need* to start over

There's the Marina
Very tidy   orderly
        the harbor master must be very good at his job

Find the perfect place to hide from tsunamis
Belonging to a faith of miles and miles

What happened to you?
Oh, yes   general anesthesia   *that* happened
        in a world that's fair
        one in which *everyone* has had a chance
                to hear E Minor's Brahms
                and leisurely   the better to concentrate

The Old Navy Base loop
The perfect sequel to coffee
        or rosolio
And it seems to me
                the marriage of raisins and brandy
                is not unlike *other* unions
                                and adjustments

And it also seems
        whatever slows down the jazz age
                lets the trumpets sound better
                and then more smoothly can the sax sing to us

Let jazz interpret the scenery
Wailing a contrary Brahms
        Brahms gone awry and radioactive

Destination?
Well, it all depends on longevity and trickery
Remembering highway 36 elsewhere
        and a fool's errand to Red Bluff
        in late March and still plenty of snow on the heights

Swerving mostly
        and twisting in and out of watersheds
                appraising fires past
                tiring well before halfway

Thinking the betrayal of love
                        is definitive treason
                        no matter the country
After which even war seems a mere recreation

Those bridges

A prolongation of letter "R"
     the straight street out of town gone
     over *water* gone
"R" as extended life
"R" for recovery
"R" for anything the eighteenth letter comes to stand for

If you're asking
     what was the very next thing that happened
        after this delay
          it would be a question in vain
For this crossing to Samoa
     was the closest thing to a true timeout

Like someone abducted by a zealous crew of E.T.s

It might be best to dig down   *really*
In the day   with a window
     an early window
     when windows were not fully understood

How the avalanche of light is let in
The letter "R" part of a purr
     that spans the bay   Humboldt called
We'll see Fairhaven, too
Take photographs for later

Spring has unleashed a wanton retrospect
     proving melancholia to be somewhat dangerous
        like End Time prophecies

There's Daby Island right
And Woodley Bar left
     at the edge of the Eureka Channel
     lefter   leftmost
        the inner reach
        the outer

I'll stay a foreigner feigning no knowledge of the bay
Or that Eureka was a Gold Rush transport center
As a non-resident dwells on appearances
     free to do this with no routine to tell

Why is Tuluwat Island a no-go zone?

A massacre   the Wiyots   the men were away
         women and children
                  no one was punished
Something awful in 1860
While clouds were filling the sky

Unbeknownst to busy mankind
Look skyward   give it personal attention

I think that before Arcata's comprehended
         there will be the streets and bridges of Eureka
                  these islands and blue-painted houses
                  these various channels and sloughs

Wait it out
Wait until a new world order obtains
Delay Arcata
         as though its postponement
                  were tantamount to stopping the clock

An orchestrated pause
         comprised of jazz and Johannes
         their improbable affinities
Eucalypts   the Australian tree   a foreign grove

No accident
No bird's beak transported the seed
                  a mental state
                  state of massacre
The roller coaster mind amends the sense of things
A surfeit of channels the currents alleging history

Imagining the course an unpaddled kayak might take
         and how long drift
         Arcata Bay to Humboldt
                  to hazard an exit
The watchful Caspian tern aloft
And the Black Brant   hovering

Three bridges to Samoa taken
To Fairhaven after that
Or Manila   another eastern Pacific conjuration
         whose cottages thrive in the scruffy dunes

There's a tower
  like the base for a windmill's blades
    an offhand construction
    quite left alone and wanting use
      any
      sad usage, even

What ovation may begin now the North Spit's attained!
What pontes rewarded with arrival!
And though the Brahms still has a way to go
  and his E Minor persists
    it's close enough for jazz to sound welcome

Let it be an interrupted serenade
Save the rest for Cagney
  he might show up
  or the surgeon
    having followed the patient to Eureka

To keep an eye on him
Going far past any Kaiser plan
Going rogue and wandering after
  like an anxious wife
    above and beyond any post-op politeness
    or cursory inspection of bandages and stitches

It was the perfect set of bridges for one-handed

Hurry!
Though with wet weather caution
  and the hypervigilance of escapees

Believe in the road and belong
  undulant yourself speculative
    a prisoner who found his way out of Pelican Bay
    and will celebrate with a joint outside the joint

Willing to chuck the sobriety that teaches furlough

If you feel confined
  get out the maps
    buy a car
      get a CC Radio for late night
And loop slowly to Arcata

As foreigner in love with houses painted blue

Prelude dwellings
Don't look for me
Though I would hear your complaints
        they are too familiar
        like a normality based on too much control

For the present magic to continue
For the creeks to flow
For the beds to be made
        and prepared for post-surgery
            we're all mostly lapsing into slumber

And the cessation of note-taking
And being ever ready to rule the world
Tucked in for the night
        yet wishing to be better known

Like a Brahms lullaby
                symphonic
                austere
                    as befits reassurance
                            there's a world that's fair
And full of simple errands run
        on windy roads
        slowly mastered

Eyes' windows understood as movies of End Time
            channeling the inner
            the outer
                    reaches

BREAKDOWN SOUTH OF CRESCENT CITY

I remember

The '57 Chevy
  that was almost brand new
    came to a stop
    in the same colored-green rain forest as now
Somewhere going away from
Or coming *to*
  the crescent of Crescent City and all its boats

My piano teacher's car
Perpetually new
He said he just kept getting new ones
  a system every three years a new one

His way of getting around
And he and I had certainly been doing that
  ever since Seattle
  traveling Eisenhower's highways to California

To San Francisco
  where lived his mother

I was told I could be part of the visit if I didn't make trouble
Well, I didn't
  but the brand new Chevy *did*
Trouble enough to stop us
    somewhere along this road
    right *here* perhaps

It just died and would not further go
Would not allow any more vacation
     until its needs were met

High above the beaches
  where the road was windy
    and you made big turns right
    and big turns left
      my teacher was patient

He didn't swear though he *was* a marine

The delay was nothing
    just a sad story of engines
    and losing control of time and distance

I could barely imagine what was wrong with the thing
He later said it was "the points"
The points!
I was fourteen
    preoccupied with puberty
      "The points?"

The term was incomprehensible!

In the program of listening
    that was my youthful apprenticeship
      I couldn't hear it all
      but I knew he needed help
A garage and a mechanic
A *tow* may have happened
    but none of this is available memory

Being stuck was all
A *metaphor* was all
The way happenstance mimics a zen timeout
    in the tall, tall trees
    with the noisy drafts between
The closest to meditation I could get

That's the way you do it
    serendipity
    breakdown
      abeyance

We'd come from the Oregon Caves back there
The cavern was guided and partly explained
We'd wandered around the creepy stalagmites
    and stalactites
      while being told the difference

But fifty years later I still don't know
    which one's the word for the downward dagger
    and which means the upward impaler

Both spikes we saw   some of them joined

and stopping the drip, drip, drip altogether
    putting an end with a final drop

The guide said, "Don't touch!"
If you *did*
    bad things would happen to the limestone

When the lecture was over the sun was too
Being just a glow to the west
So that we really didn't exactly reenter the daylight
    but rather entered a bigger
    far *larger* cave
      and there'd be no guide at all

When the Chevy conked out
When we were still shy of San Francisco
      by hundreds of miles
    I thought,
      "I'm tired of dependence
      tired of machines
      and grownups
      and knowing I'd have to be one someday
        keep a car running
        keep a *job* going!"

I thought like a bat in broad daylight

Gave up   tried not to complain too much
But couldn't resist, "When do we get there?"

He laughed
Turned teacher and said,
    "One day you'll be driving a pink Cadillac
    if you work hard
    that means the piano, my friend!"

There were a lot of "my friends" in his teaching
During the lessons,
    "Listen," he'd say
    "you're scratching the surface, my friend!"

But it was never an insult
Rather   it seemed a secret told
    you felt that   with his help

you'd discover whatever it was
that was under that surface

He made it intriguing
I'd keep scratching
hoping I'd find it
without a breakdown of my own
as prodigy or otherwise

I think he would have told me to quit the piano
Think he believed in me
After all he'd previewed down under already
the caves
like a mastery possible

REDWOOD HIDEOUT

Just off the highway
      that highway waits
          on a hermit
         a refugee
            a fugitive

Where the minimal turnout's annexed
      to an overgrown track
      some long unused forest road
                contouring down

Here is where you might hide away
A monk of nothing in particular
Debts paid
      at least the ones you remember
Music played
      at least the Polonaises of Frederic
         the musical scores having been donated

With the *Scrabble* dictionary committed to memory
As well as names
      the names of all the attendees at Burning Man in 1997
      and the pets they brought with them

Yes!   right here!
For the rest of this night
      and henceforth
      unobserved except by the owls
Right here would rituals in solitude be enacted
        and the terrible story of *Aida* sung

And this will be enough to attempt in the redwoods
In the rain
      and the wind
        remembering with you
        though you are distant
Way down deep reviewing affection!

If you love me, lovely woods
      I won't be afraid to stay on
        for I know it's a road that never ends

its winding down this way and that

And if it were followed I should be *also*
As some *avant-garde* resistance
    when the guerilla fighter fades into the jungle
    just for the sake of doing so

Without tactics   or strategies
A risk-free trial
    enjoying the sunless color green
            and all its shades

Be an explorer
A slow motion choo-choo
    learning the route that suits
    the subject of pedology
            however long it takes
The behavior and development of children to study
Pressure on to reach conclusions

It is a high quality forest
And the light there is that lights the way
    is true to chlorophyll's imperatives

And with the scent of moistured soil and soft rain
You wonder
    how long have ferns adorned the planet
            ferns and all their variant designs
            delicate
                outblessing with aesthetic lacework

The whole scene lending itself to *pavane*
The stately dance to go with the redwoods' stage set

Things going wrong in all other places
And being unlucky all of one's life
    still this off-road hillside is compensatory psyche
            restorative
            a wonderful secret!

Slipping further into seclusion
    you can see the features of a hillside grotto
    yet always stay
            philosophically

in the background

Witness to a seance held by the forest
The *ouija* of all those branches' intentions
        swirling in the updrafts

One hour so far and the monk is accustomed
The coast has meaning
        that returns him to *other* solitudes
                well before the world required sanctuary

Returns him to shinier landscapes
        poulticing
                there is not much value left
                for we had moved too far in front of history
                        and haunted what was to come

There was too much theory
We gave permission to the gods
        invited them
                to intervene
                        for we would not pray for anything

And what words were used to accomplish as much
        were mostly complaints
                that everything has a way of taking forever

There are water spirits
They are benign
        without a program of destruction

The turnout and trail were elements of portal
The edge of an aura vast as all the highlands
As teetotaler you seek an award, perhaps
        for all that sobriety a day-at-a-time
                surely a specific reward is possible

The bark ahead   anthropomorphic
        the face of a demon fading with the daylight
        face rearranged by premonition
But I've lost any fear of suggestive imagery

Even *darkness* I don't mind
The act of possession

having occurred already in an undisclosed age

Listen!
     listen!   at one with the whispers
There is even music without a philharmonic prerequisite!

Each moment a picture of the next
And prejudices
     and all impulsive decisions
          are examined for their potential disturbance
And then   with some bemusement
     abandoned in favor of gray-blue stillness

There may be someone *else* off-road and preceding
     but I think not
The way I proposed too purposeless
     for even the Dalai Lama to take an interest

And certainly no following is in the offing
It took extra effort to stop
     for 101 was curving most agreeably
     its banks just right
          a simulated landing
          performed by a lazy airplane
               in loopy descent to the land of tidal waves

And to arrest that glide
     while one's ears were popping
     and there were prospects for chowder
That took some rebellion
And belief
     that the hideaway was dividend glade
          and analog of learning

Stop!
Watch the trees as if they're prehistoric
     feeling prehistoric your *own* self
          with no knowledge of engines
          and the oil that facilitates their pistons' cycles

Stop!
To be a shadow
     and advocate of unseen virtuous action
A final phone call home

perhaps leaving out your commitments

Invisible Crescent City is none the wiser
For there were no Robert Frost "promises to keep"
And while there "may be some mistake" in it
        I think the greater mistake
                would be to stay a creature of the highway

For you know by now
        that travel is an operetta's daydream
        and undeserving of indefinite and serious study

The car can be caroche
An artcar   immoral
But the roadside
        is a place for Ebenezer Scrooge to unravel
                without having to atone
                        for in the absence of Bob Cratchit
                        and "God bless us every one!"
                                his ill temper sublimates

His executive control eased up on
Even the book come calling
        as anagram title
        threatening to be anything you please
                a plasmoid of moving on
                one place to another
Without a journey between

There is already a tingling sensation
It goes with disappearance
                        without saying
                        without a clue
                                and reneging

You couldn't *possibly* keep all those promises anyway

What happens when a paradigm shifts
Where the neglected logging road has turned to lustring
And the moss
        is a glossy supplemental silk supply
                and offering
                when losing one's mind is no big deal

The loser assuaged
And signed up for a newer, better mind
        based on listening alone
            the wild rose like a hypnotherapy
            the search for acumen
The *accidental* brain
                in search of science's many fictions

Believing you belong sequestered
As any book
        shelved in a superlative library
            more absolutely lasting
                than Alexandria's
                with the Pharos beaming somewhere

The Ptolemys' bloodlust held in check
            albeit barely
            with great difficulty
The weapon of the mind averse
Its opposition pronounced as these whereabouts
Something cold as carpet bombing
                anti-precision's masterpiece

The Saint George Reef
        in charge of its own Promethian bonfire
More offshore than ever
Yet connected to the near in unexpected ways

No one was harmed in the making of this solitude
        the benefits immediately noticeable
        as a certain mobile awareness
                    not confined to the mind

The unremarkable turnout and trail
        like a quarrel between sylvatic and aquatic
Gray light's perfection
            outlining acquaintanceship with vast spaces

And   Goddamn!
All the music of Rich Ferguson
        is learned for later
        listening   with time for seconds
            for the whole opera of his art

And he'd said,
"No one stays around for very long"

But then he said he'd wait for *you*!
         yes   right here   wait for you
                  definitely
                  roadside

And may someone *else* wait
The way Rich is saying,
                         "Wait   *further* wait"
               means it's likely

All of L.A. gathered in barely a clearing
Turns out there's plenty of room amidst the seedlings
         and since L.A. became a concentrate
         we will attend the city's essence
                  the seventh degree of E Flat Major
                  in repeated dips from the tonic
                         for a minimalist enthrallment

Stepping all over
         knowing something of the lives of others
         in a southland mural and cinerama
And the turnout   though an introduction
                  sufficed for *satori*

The redwoods' *ortho* represented
         the mists dampening the locofoco such
                  the loss of daylight's accepted
                  like a single note in lieu of a symphony

Funny
         it's only been the briefest stay
         but the car has thoroughly rusted
                  and is resting for the forseeable
Right there   its last position in space-time

The lemures of ancient Rome have shut their emotions off
In their afterlives   they are dispassionate

They have not restricted their haunting to The Seven Hills
         but ghost these heights so far from the Tiber
         as though these woods were wellspring forest

and spirits draw sustenance
are influenced to *stabilize* their hauntings

So empty space is an agreeable medium
And I can be a parent now   finally
Though patricide should follow the ferns
        their exquisite matrices
                Thanatos
                the forest
                    how it lures!
Like automatic dreams
        recurring
        recountable
                all inconspicuous compartments known

The Palace of Sleep has its doors wide open

You think of the dawn redwood
A deciduous tree
How different it is from these coastal evergreens!
        losing foliage
            long ago   some divergence

Staged a feint
But we know its redhood heart knew better
        no Chinese tree on path to nether seed
Speak past the fossil
Seek   like water   the lowest level
        and explanation

I availed myself of damp kindling
        and a reading room of twisting branches
For now the biosphere is this enclosure
Like a boat in a bubble of froth
        in the presence of creator gods
        blissful

They speak French   "*Bonjour*!"
French   "*Ecoute*!"
French   "*Le vent, le vent, ecoute*!"

What could I say back, eliding?
What could I be behind the scenes?

Keep the pages dry you'd fill with fragile script
The ink will run its blue propaganda

My piano teacher will celebrate my independence
        and perhaps cease his refrain,
            "You're scratching the surface, my friend!"

He always wanted slow practice
Well, slow practice he will *have*!
I'm certain he sees this success in depth
        and the piano touch that goes with it

A temperate rain forest
There are only a few places you find them
        adjusted downward for civilization

Is it any less precious than silver?
Work in the fields?

Give something of yourself to sylvan realms
For the rest of this day go deeper into the timbered jungle
        and let's be clear:
            there is plenty of time for that
                the internet dissolving a byte at a time

The electronic universe of off-on and yes-no
Black-and-white reimagined
        as a million cries of just one waly!

Perhaps a late night talk show later
Dry in a waterproof poncho
        the storm music made and built to suit the coziest court

You really want to go after this
        with a secret terrible delight
                that dishonesty's arrested
                held in check
And with newfound virtue spell the letters of truth slowly

Over and over till the unconscious takes over
Thinking *safety*
        safety unto you and yours
                                in the redwood groves

The term "roadside" returned to a peaceful meaning
Free of explosives
  no IEDs
    land mines
      or trip wires

A Lost World acquired
Fay Wray and King Kong
I'm growing up
  even now
    past the sixty-fifth year of cells

I'm a lunarian
  descended to earth and its oceans
I'll make a report and be raptured back
After a thorough reconnaissance
  of the evil done on the oxygen world
    that was so unproductive!

And which
  for all its feverish exploits
    could not accomplish a thing

I'm throwing my money away
The pockets are empty
Gave green to green
  the dollars fluttering and whirling away
It is startling to realize just how paper-thin were its promises

I want to get into this
And you you want this as well
  no average subject

But I am weakening with hunger
A downturn
  a recession
If you were running the show
    what crumbling before you raised the alarm
    and rebuilt paradise in such a way
      no depression may visit?

The crystal ball is spherical green
The canopy curling
  with meaningful trigonometry

a global chlorophyll convergence

And I am walking in slight rain
    on a path leading down to Somewhere's dens

CRESCENT CITY: POSTLUDE TO AN AFTERMATH

Close to the restaurant the tsunami's imagined

And everywhere there's evidence
Wood chips   seaweed   and stones

The tsunami said it did nothing wrong
        for it had no moral sense to work with
        owned up to that
Might have had the best of intentions, even
Sloshing about
            if it had any intentions at all

The water was onstage flowing
        to a distant seismic drum
        with long-reaching beats
            half a day's delay
            yet soon enough for flimsy boats

"Put out!
Put out!
Be safe at sea
        beyond the shallow fathoms' runup!"

And some were able

Close to the restaurant's doors
        the burden of proof is spilled
        where the water ran   a remnant mud
Drainage like a crime scene needing detectives

It would have been ebb and flow
And Crescent City had waited
            patient
            stoic
                until an equilibrium came back to town
Until the monster from subduction died

Its reign a planetary summons
Dialing the number
        that connects you
            to all of pandemonium's compartments

Now   in the rainy-windy aftermath
Talk!
        talk to anyone!
                find witnesses!
And then
        with a fresh set of batteries
                begin to have it your way
                                with firsthand

A respectful, gentle listener
With a mic to capture and document
An inquiry like the flood that came
        in slow motion though
                from waitress
                to cop
                to sheriff
                to skippers
                        to yester's bystanders

You'll lay your hands on the wreckage
See the ships that survived
        and otherwise craft
                                tilting
                                half-and-half immersed

You will see the harbor close-up
Hear the stories
        yeah   be a good listener if you really want to know
Rooted in timeout
Let timeout be in charge of all dialogue
        the better to balance curiosity and delirium

A local you must be for this sad, sad Tuesday
        and maybe more than that

What happened that happened faraway
        shook the dome of the Pacific
                Japan itself barely defended
Prostrate when a river of all of the sea ran inland

River as wide as the north and the south

And that sudden super Amazon

was Neptune unhinged
his tantrum spreading faster than a jet plane's travel
    to the eastern walls of his ocean
Dense with small craft

Yet behold!   the American restaurant!
Free of consequence
    owing to a certain height above the freak show
        and now serving survival on a bun!

There should be an intro
But the only one that will do
    must be an encyclopedia of this place
    the summary of all that'sgone before

With minutiae
The waves big and small just a part of it
We must have it all
    and through context take the town's pulse

The sea is circular
Rounded
    an invitation to the Pacific to overflow
    and make a bay beyond the map

People are drawn to the quiet crescent
    its being psychoactive
Proceed yourself to the harbor now
    encountering those who found the emperor
        knocking on their door
        so long after the *Missouri* signing
            in victorious September of '45

Long time passing
Until this imperial tsunami
Like the *avant-garde* of Co-Prosperity's retro Sphere
    inexorable the wave front
    the invasion a clinic for ambition itself
        the ocean itself dumbed down and subservient

Even Neptune knows his monster's beyond his godly control
    and threatens his throne!

How many have died who thought safety a foregone?

What assumptions unnerved and too lately renounced?

It was suicide traveling west to east
Where complaisance is a death wish
And needing an extraordinary introduction
        a paternalistic tide
        like a massive discipline
                after which the boats are bent and splintered vessels

Where was the caution that should follow us?
That guardian prudence?
Best to assume that havoc's entwined
        with every occasion for yawning

Let us see and hear what tectonic tricks were played
And continue a struggle to understand
        as if our reeducation were at hand
        bad habits turned 'round
                and recertified as virtue

We are formally charged with gang affiliation
Where the homeboys are hostage to collective ennui
"I am weak but the group is strong"
        the refrain more rote than conviction

Walk the citizens' dock
As much a fool yourself as any pretender to wisdom
        having thoughts of a wife
        for whom you would now most assuredly respect
If allowed

Remembering the adage,
"What your partner does is none of your business"
And not only *that*, but
"What *you* do is none of your business!"
And not only *that*, but
"What *everyone* does is beyond your purview"

And then   as a happier witness
        having the sense and genius of a stone
        doing nothing with its perfect zen mind
A kind of altruism kicks in

Proceed   ask questions

There's a dock in shambles
    and nothing to be done until the cranes appear
    but it hasn't kept the authorities away
        uniforms are everywhere

There's a swim spot swamped and wanting attention
They must be especially aggressive
        to restore the industry
        the commerce of fishing

And so
    on this citizens' dock
        be journalist
        chronicler
        inquisitor
            producer and director
Planting subliminal messages in all I ask
Though all I ask for seems innocent assessment

There's plenty to see
The Marine Supply
Del Norte sheriffs in a keep-away stance
    the aftermath an obvious crime scene
        where Nature's the perp
        unapprehendable

The officers said they'd been posted there
Said they saw a lot of what took place
So what exactly *did* take place?
    what physics?
    the exact oscillations of the ocean?
        what specifically happened?

Never mind
You'd have to drug an oceanographer
    get him to talk
        with a truth serum or something
            threaten to take away a grant
If you wanted *definitive* replies

For now the town is obsessed with recovery
    it's natural

The bay's bottom was bare between floods

Really!   that's a lot of tsunami then!
    a good old fashioned sloshing about
        the infrastructure set upon
        like uncertain times

The way the harbor's shaped there was nowhere to go
There was a big "in" and just as big "out"

"Surveys have shown we have six sunken vessels
    that was once a sailboat
    the *Bountiful* there is a big steel-hulled boat
        that was lifted up
        and brought down hard
            on everything around it

"Over there on Anchor Way
    the pier was torn and tossed
The wave just pulled things up and flung them
The floating dock
    that was styrofoam encased
        totally destroyed

"There are divers having a look
They're working right now"

The woman who spoke was Fish and Game
And she was fairly breathless recounting this
    and the evacuations

"If it hits on a high tide we're done,"
    said a man who lived on his boat
There were a few others doing the same
"Any aftershocks, you hope it's low tide
    they almost evacuated twice today!"

They were recounting Alaska
The wave from that state broke in the moonlight
'64 it was
    and it scared the hell out of everyone

The lighthouse couple who saw it all
    thought for sure they'd die on the island

For hours the show went on

And sea caves
      never seen before
            were seen in the ebb
            before each run-up
They stayed in an altered state for the duration

And they were *very* married then
As if at first
      when the wedding was a brand new bonding
A lot of information devolved
      from their magnificent endurance

Well, they recut the cake
            and it was sweet indeed
            as was their survival!

Now in broad daylight
      the network of witness
            was a special shared frequency of concern
I must make sure to set it down
How the sea beat the shore and all its isles
      its thousands of windows smashed

As wide a river as all of north-south
            and searching inland if it could

You can say that you will study it
A retrospective   *good!*
And *do* reflect
      that not *if*
      but *when* Cascadia slumps
            and its rolltop desk descends
                  the Pacific's contents will certainly spill
And in its birthday suit drown us all
Like ancient aliens
      all liquid and merciless

A specific date
Something bigger
      brought on by hydrogen   oxygen
      the two gases joined improbably
            to be a molecule of malice
            with others of its kind

And this universe of water to come
          akin to the Indian Ocean's upbraiding
          no one knowing there had been offense
It told its story best at Aceh   accusatory
That energy reserved for inflicting oblivion

What will be the argument
          in Oregon
                  California
Waiting in the dock to hear the charges
The Crescent especially found guilty
And the gods warring to punish
                                  with expert witnessing

Crescent City's harbor is calm right now
                            well-lit
We have stepped out of fear and are rogatory
          the wind a beautiful fan in place

Accompanied   alone
This reporter
          for an hour
                  is paid by the minute
                          for the sight of haphazard hulls

And authority's a moviedom
And posing in lieu of something to do
          their uniforms mostly dark green
          a race of plant people   uprooted
A human potential movement
                  well-breakfasted
                  their official vehicles shiny as spacecraft

And there's gratitude extreme chaos stayed away

They are milling   reflective
The latest news from Japan
          non-binding
                  but carefully apprised
                          survival training underway

Now, the man who went to sea and safely floated
          miles from nowhere
          found a Cat Stevens solution

With a Willy Wonka's magic ticket
He's Hemingway's old man in limbo
    rocked and cradled
    and he spends some *time* out there

No surprise the water was calm
He was beyond the drag of the tsunami near-shore
Put himself to work again too
    the fish and the fisherman

And far enough from the harbor at Crescent
    he even imagines
        beyond the peace of deep water
        some balance
            an equilibrium restored to the blue world

Freedom installed and monitored for devils
He's learned a lot
    and become *staunch*
        with the knowledge the sea has lent

And   out there
    having passed between the white lighthouse
    and the last defensive forts of headland
        he bested the continental shelf
        positioned his craft wisely
            above deep submarine canyons

Far, far from Humboldt Bay too
            its shallow concerns

It's possible
    that not only the Japanese wave
        but *every* vexation is distanced
And the things he knows are different
        from the awkward crackle of ship-to-shore

He had changed what was coming
    over the green and textured ocean
Did something *before* the happening
And the sea being more of the planet than land
    he thinks he'll stay out
    stand off the land's minority surface

He will join the company of mermaids
Drink rain from the buckets
     beyond the reach of landlubber religions
        and their irrelevant virgins

He is threading the reef and all the rocks to St. George
Proud of his navigation
     a sea scientist without portfolio
     linking back to the trireme and later caravels
        history in his timbers

Thinking of the poem, "Marina," by T.S.
     he's neither rich nor poor
     union or non
        and a brand new vocabulary's come with deliverance

How the world works is liquid
A tutelage not always gentle
And what ballet that's in it's like the long swell
     and how the hull plies crest and trough

His friends are a guarantee he *will* return
Tie up   and have some beers

It is a *shared* slowing down
A company of pitch and roll
     port and starboard
        how the continent cannot stop
        but must submit to eternal motion

And so   in *exquisite* communion
     they'll talk
        and remark the strangeness of solid earth
        the pleasant absurdity of firmament
          if that is what it truly is

Oh!   timely departure!
Let me be your crew of one acolyte
     detached and eager to help with the catch
In time I will learn not to overwind the winch
And not too romantically conceive never-never tangents

I'd bring an instrument onboard
Take a little time to relax

While the waves are tidal
        a recital at sea
        the concert to include salt air

How the word "infidel" is meaningless
Just the two of us in an existential trawler
        remembering that history's inclusive
            and likes natural phenomena

So I say it's a BCE sea
        and memorable for all of that
In some excellent century
            will some forlorn Atlanteans
                admit they should have built their city
                    in the basin of the safe Pacific?

There, its architecture might have been spared
        from the kleptomaniac deep

Some lady love in town
        desires the fisherman also remember
            not the ancient times
            but her present mastery of pot roast
                not to mention blueberry muffins

After all
        though the boat was in danger
            it's really this woman he can't live without

Whatever charisma he's privy to
        that *too* is something for study
And I   his apprentice   hope and desire to find it out
        thriving with his offshore

Richter 9.0   9.6   could there ever be a 10?
The earth's cleverness expanded
        while the lurdans among us
            stumble in response to the tremors

The daydream of fishing over
        I'm inclined to steal the sheriff's 4x4
        and drive away to poverty south
To reenter the landlubber city
                    of not too hot

                              not too cold

To a room temperature metropolis
        thoroughly moderate in every way
Learning new languages never intended to be spoken

To South of Market to settle in doorways
Detached and waiting to see what will happen

Del Norte at large
        all the laws of diminishing returns
                enforced through hypnosis
                and the memory of Ali Akbar Khan
He once said he wanted to start a school of music on the moon
After everyone's learned the sarod on earth

There's still time to lyricize
        disaster to the living
        disaster to the dead

This American city   Crescent
        not so long after the peak of empire
                struggles to say it's grateful
                though the party's past
And birth rates promise a fiercer future

When being brave will mean something new
Untested mettle awash in riches powerless to spend

Even the light of day is helpless
                for relief is a prayer repeated

I'm entering hangover in spite of abstinence
Even a culture that gets it right
                must slide into the sea

And though its sails are hanked
        still a free-floating anxiety commences
As if listening to wartime radio
A comedy, perhaps
                when
                from time to time
                    is heard:

"Brought to you by grief"

Tsunami as publicity
Nature's "spot"   and promotion
            the science channel chock full

We know the earth is deep space too
And it's E.T.'s wave train we saw
                home security in the offing
Rampage as crackdown
            where complaisance is arrested
            and Gaia's made a person of interest

This aftermath
This intro
      with prelude
            and postlude
                  enters the encyclopedias
                        as if we could have it all
                        write it all down as documentary sonata

Everyone will listen
Well-rounded with crescents

Go slowly to the harbor
      lost as you want to be
      but *careful* lost
Proceed to a virtual emperor and say:

"The sea is rising
      though you are not to blame
            and co-prosperity's in place
            and spanning east and west"

Long time passing
That minifies and morphs its atrocities
      gone to bed with each occasion for evil

I am changed
Bad habits organized
      for reeducation
            by see-and-hear monsters with gangland affiliation

"I am weak but the group is strong…"

The tsunami less frightening with solitude
Public opinion serving only to diminish its beauty
Such a *restive* ocean
        that spilled its basin
                the water planet jostled

Early in the interviews
        you know that "in depth"
                must include the god of the sea
                but so far he's mum

He's not talking
Though all I ask
        is why he took the job in the first place

Perhaps Neptune's obsessed with his own recovery
And second-guessing his deeds

SUNSET BAY

See it there
A sunset just a darkening

A black-and-white affair more suitable for bad guys
        for lonesome times

It is said the rocks were blasted
At the entrance to the bay
            sticks of dynamite were used
            you didn't stick around!
Unless you wanted to die

The stock market's crashed again
It's 1933
        and the sun has simply turned to stone with the times
An amorphous gray is all

It's still a market's sunset
But what we're hearing
        like banshee landlords
            are the cries of the avifauna
            their absolute agenda

The bay like a sudden crater you come to
When the truth about money is a costly surprise
        the color of steel
        the new color of the sinking sun

A new gray
        as if gray were some anomaly
            what painters' eyes have never seen
Their palettes' bright ouija instigating poverty

The ranger's pronounced it in government green
        that seems another version of "All is lost!"

Chances are you own a uniform yourself
And keep it tailored to a life form's vanishing point

Money markets' alliteration only
A tease in the mind

a cork afloat in the *cranial* sea
where no horizon's discerned
     and one goes dimeless into winter
Something not thought of before
              upwind or down

We're just about turned to animals again
No one's to blame
    and how does it feel
       half-light and half-dark?
It's a sunset devoured by battleship gray
And waiting on sirens of Roman numeral wars
      World Wars   I   II
      and counting impatiently

Let that ranger speak
Can purple at least be a color at Sunset Bay?
Can we hope for red?
    right now?   maybe not
The westmost smithereens a blown apart temple
And deconstructed with extreme prejudice

Can the bay be a sky?
Something accomplished by a paint-by-numbers showoff?
    what sea life does

The ranger's talking science all the time
To no one in particular
    talking to retire
    she incubates a bias towards the west
       the last lines of sight beginning to curve
       and be a reservoir of sable numerology
         realized in a shallow bay

The ritual sun tries the day
    in a court of Pluto's underlings
    in the moustached dark
Unseen watchers watching the unseen

Back-of-the-eyeball night oncoming
Its preface of forties earnestness
           and far-flung funny business
Those eyes we saw in the war books' pages
On all the trains to confinement

Heard the Seven Devils were more than those truncated bluffs
The ones you see from Cape Arago
Devils traveling long-distance to plunder
     steal spirits
     their long hair heinous

They would drive you crazy if they could!
And there were no signs to say so
     what's next
        or in how many years hence!

This is home for now, nevertheless
Live at home here   Sunset Bay
     with a writing pad and pen
        a cup of salt water
        and words

"Ranger!   I would speak with you
You said in your lecture you'd answer any question
Say everything you know for sure
     how your ranger's hat's creases came to be
        and what shores are these you faithfully patrol"

Her uniform is perfect cover
     though she is otherwise awkward
A local constable you ask
        to hear the dynamite blast once again
        that would have echoed to Arago
           the Cape
           and the man for whom
To wherever he lives now

If this were the east it would be Brooklyn
Rhythmic as all this sunset city of waves
     a last hour's oasis

It's someone else's bay
One hand in my pocket
     it's a good place to start drinking again
Be in opposition to pundits
        who busy themselves with pancake makeup
        as if taking a course in look-good

Where's AA?
Well, it only takes two drunks for a meeting
        according to that good book of Bill's
                as he sees it

I'll ask the ranger if she wants to have a meeting
If she's a friend of Bill's
        the code query sneaking up
        letting desperation
                check you out of this T. S. reality
                that the poet said we can only take so much of

Those of us that are human, that is
There was *that* qualification

It may be a case of too much time   free time
Time it takes for a sun's light   however feeble
        to be done with lighting
        to be entirely *under*
                the way the ancient elephant
                turtle
                or Atlas
                        understood the concept

Guess where the day is scissored from the night
        from the rest of your dream
See it there!   the bay of fallen currency
It's a flat screen's picture
        the rest of our lives if we don't look out

A fifties' television's test pattern sky
A wrongful Ides of March for a gay pride parade
        that turns its back
        on "The Importance of Earnest Being a Nothingness"

And Oscar Wilde lies in wait
Like a squall to westward
        Dorothy's rainbow in tatters
                and no longer an option

Oh!   the sunset there *may* be
The colors it *could* be made of
        behind the walls of the sea that Mozart built

Be grateful sound has no dependent prism
No spectrum that's all-weather   all-terrain
This is why the boombox came along
        to accompany the bay
                its nearby forest
                    the ranger's flat affect
                        and all imaginary companions

The light is leaking away into Hades
No mirror may capture now and later
        nor telescope's lens espy the shade
Gloom itself is leached for a Cinerama's darkness

A 12-pack's worth of morbid hops
        the set of the sun missed entirely
        unless a dimming day is bay enough

It seems the end of everything
There's only Madonna
        and small creatures who don't think too much
Today has Alaska and its Kodiak come to roost
            the shroud of Novarupta woven by Ingmar
                in a wind chill of gloom

Ranger Katherine's girl's shown up
She's grown   has no accent
        though she's journeyed from Europe just months ago
        as escapist daughter
                her best frock
                a gift of the state of mind of Oregon

The sunset's in search of better painters
Wants a Fauvist's attention paid
Wants acquaintanceship with color
        for want of a prism the bay stays gray

Look more closely   renew a vigil westward
        the sunset dressed in mummy rags
                do you believe it?
                    red's attempted seduction in progress
                        in spite of opacity

No doubt you are anxious
As your mother and father were

as they contemplated Germany's intentions
Or Khrushchev was
    the big baby-bye
       having spread himself too thin
       like this home-sweet fog-of-war atmospheric lie

It is a brainwashed sky
The bride ranger said, "I do!"
    said,
    "I love this job
       a man   the weather"

Bring dynamite to shatter this monochrome expanse again!
For it's strung out
    a bar room bay
       just the bones
       and the bones told, "Begone!"
They don't care the symphony ends with tarnished cymbals

And postcards must replace this sea
Strangely demure yet overexposed
    low tide   neap tide
       the surf slips away
         doesn't feel the same about the shore
The tuxedoed sun at a black-and-white ball

A pearly smearing like metamorphosed dreams
The key in the cracks
    of pianoforte love
    for lonesome bad guys
       on the shores of a puzzle bay interlocking

Guest color
Guest texture

"After my husband died I took this job
Rainy days I'd do a puzzle
    I had puzzle vision
       next thing you know it all interlocks
       nerve endings hard-wired to *nuage gris*"

The gray of Omaha
AA neutral
    all that plays peekaboo

with ordinary primary wheels of colored pies

Change this world for this scenery!
The End become becoming!
    Ice 9
        polar-brittle barrens
            and a song
            to accompany the ersatz mind?

Doesn't-matter mind's coma clouds
What takes away internal organs to la-la
The color *retreat* is made of
        or an expression of Edith Piaff
        twisted to regret

Some higher grade of black
Some *devil* come 'round
        one of those Seven
            whose faces face the sea of ships

Truncation's bluffs
Erosion's clays and passions
        cliffs as *portraits* south of foggy Arago
The huge house of whales and seals
Say to a friend
        the befriending sea attends Love's afterwards wilderness

A sunset just a darkening
A State Park for bad guys in search of a snitch
        whose guest appearance at police headquarters
            has compromised their operations

They'll need extra help
If this were Illinois
        they'd use the services of the ghost of Mister Capone

The end of a Children's Crusade!
That's what this is!
        if this is The Levant
        or wherever they went into captivity at last

You think you have to die to get to paradise
        and be delivered
            from this maundering sun

      gray as 1933 and its banshees' agenda

Seven Devils strong
     no dynamite can make them leave
     no prayer can halt their perfect hysteria
        where they haunt with their own specious wailing

It is the truth about money they tell
Its color and sky a nightmare painter's studio
     the painter made a ranger
        with a palette all of government green
        and useful idiots
           born to blend into its wavelength
Chances are they succeed

Entered their heads and stayed mental thereafter
     souls for sale

Chances are they sold out corks afloat
And the horizon just a theoretical division

Whatever sunsets have been
Whatever boulevards of light beheld
     they have entered history like a coloring book
        on a cold, cold day of gray unthought of

A young girl's Saturday alone with a puzzle
     whose squiggles each are backside ashen cardboard
     no matter the butterfly of the front-and-center portrait

Sunset Bay is a jigsawn picture face down
While we watch and turn into animals
     paint-by-numbers divisible by 2
        the number of the last World War
        that saw the debut of brand new sea monsters

Will show you a picture if you don't believe it
Church of the unseen west
     but soon you'll see it beginning to curve
     like Einstein's light

And Pluto's in control
Pluto and his minions

Layover Bay
        where accidents of the ritual sun
                comprise a *reservoir* of forties' funk

Be kind!
The eyes we saw   watching the watchers
        trains of devils descending
You were feeling the same way *before*
Please don't lie about it   even long-distant

I saw you at the Cape   Cape Arago
        at home and long-haired
You'd answered any question
                and were a kind constable
                at an outpost of London

If this were England it would belong to the Baskervilles
        their hound to make an appearance soon
When you'd ask to hear its howls in opposition to pundits

Darker is all
T. S. Eliot's reality show
We must be kind to *him*
        those of us that are human with too much free time

There is communion with umbrellaed day
However feeble
        its line of sight
        and scissored currency
                star in a dream tumbling westward

Place ranger's been to and wants to return to
To say she's a friend of Bill's test patterns
        and the colors they could be
                if the rain remembers how to tie a bow

Sound has not a spelling bee
In the bay like a crater of the flooded moon
Gloom itself has bought a 12-pack
        and made its own plans for sundown
                when it will sit still for its blank Cinerama

See the Chistians' precious demons at work
And say to them

their famous evil
        may only be destroyed by a *greater*
All words having become military moments

Alaska's lost some latitude in coming here
        to make a symphony of birds
        their Latin names so very appealing
And it invites the lesser magic of machines
            to rust in the twilight
            and be a stillness in the water

Aftermath of TNT
Your bones don't care
        that the monsters have come
            and are about to fall down the horizon
                in the Land of Lacrimosa

Yesterday's holidays observed
It's often said "more often in the breach than et cetera"
It's no place for valentines
        unless they're enemies in love

Guess the day of your death is celebrated
The time it takes
        to be done with the walkways of the sea

Means not waiting in line
The rest of a dream drawn out   logy
Maybe Sunset Bay's a movie never made
        blood pressure rising
            at the Grammy Awards for banshee shouts

If this were philosophy
        the mind is what's before us
            a wizened mother coma sky
The concrete screen to mask your sensibilities

"The mind has had an *accident*," the ranger whispered

Your recovery to include a theory of sunset
        that allows for visitation rights
            to this bay's pearly gray
With room for one gray whale whose mind includes your own
And all the tragicomic creative writing it caused

that is an unrequited love for the sea

Somehow the bay's this picture apology
        for not being the watery court where sunset presides
We are forced to pray for it even today
Being drowsy with gray's monomania

So swim out
Out to the dynamited reef
        what's left of it
                and with alien hypothermia lie down

The dusk disintegrates before you
Like an adolescent love
        whose obsession
        disproves the sane reflections of the virgin mind
                one month into sweet reinvented love

If this is infatuation   then darling, come here
Bring your camera body to sun the sundown
Make a promise to do this
        no matter the wind chill

Here's a frock
        to spare your shivering
                in the bay's darkened day
You're a better painting
        than the next day's automatic canvas
                all the shades that Germany knew in the fog
                ground-hugging its barroom bones

Strangely demure, do not slip into requiem now
Tarot first!
Tarot into early evening
        the cards cut   the deck divided
        with welcome precision

Nothing else matters
An act against gray such
        whatever Fate turns up
                is a firmament of contrast

If the ranger holds Mass
        for the whales in search of a bottomless sea

It is the truth to hide away their government of pods
            the sopranos among them
                        anxious for history to resume

For T. S. to renounce the mermaids
            and sing hosannas to depression
            to the truth about money

He will not be a useful idiot
            or a plaything for reticent muses
                        or enough of a bad guy
                                    to qualify for a pair of brand new trousers
But attend the Church of the Unseen Curvaceous Nihilistic

Let's talk about it
Take all the time there is
            while heavenly bodies push and pull the planet
            and tides are in and out of the bay

The sun   in absentia   awaits your eyesight
Your camera body
            what do you do?

All the scare stories ever told are sounding in the silvery air
And the refuted sun is walled up westward
            its colored clouds
                        quite gone to bed everywhere here

There's no election   no banners
            its sunset package destined for Japan
Where's Roosevelt?
What New Deal's dead in the fog?

The first space walk still years away
                                    ahead of time
Even the ranger is a disconcerted soldier
            a person of interest in all these clouds come to earth

Is she Eliot's accomplice?
Is there even a forecast?
And if there is
            may it not be a lie

And keep Pluto underground

It's bad enough
     his minions interfere with our simply taking care

It's surprisingly still for all the dynamite used
Guess it was yesterday
     is yesterday
          that melancholia sees
          in observing holidays
               and no place for Valentine's

Blood pressure raised but no sign of red
A See-It-Not State Park

STATELINE MARKET

It's closing   a shame
The store astride the borderlands

The states are fighting over you

California!
You needed this enterprise
      with all of Hollywood going for you?

Oregon!
How *dare* you covet this small business?

Extortionists!   50% off 75%   last days!

My god, do they know something?
Whoever owns it still?

Is it a very *local* Rapture they have learned of
      that will separate the citizens of Winchuck
      and spirit them away
            to unspoiled coasts beyond Beyond?

This unreasonable sale
      the signs of haste, oh yes!
There's something here besides going out of business

They're fighting over you, Stateline Market!
They're tug-of-warring
      the forces of good and evil
            add big and little
                  ancient and modern
                        somewhere and nowhere

T-shirts   gifts   kites for rent
In a yellow building on the edge of finality
All its myrtlewood displayed
      as if with repentance
            for some unknown sale

WALDPORT

i.   It Wasn't the Way Columbus Came

It wasn't the way Columbus came
The Indians this far west had a little more time
     and knew not the Taino's enslavement
     and being dragged down

From the western sea today no tsunami arises
And when the morning comes
     the croissants will freshly deliver you
        into early afternoon

Such crowds there are seem more or less dispersed
You move like a fish through the remainder
Summer-sent
     you remember being semi-rich
        in the port named for the forest

Enjoying a fantasy occupation that might come true
     before the moon falls to earth

Dance before breakfast   before discovery
Wait till you see the catamaran!
Brought all the way from seductive Florida
     and it's great for the shoals

The rain's been pouring these past few days
Writing prose the while   a minimalist prattle
     all the truth that's known to cloud cover

The emcee sun is nowhere to be found
     and has forsaken the drizzly daytime

This is not the way Cabeza de Vaca went, either
The salmon undammed for awhile

The day is soon destroyed by thought
The adult determines the remainder
The day is *distraught*
       of limited imagining

Hold tight to ritual
That which survives explorers and their passions
A car show in place of a road trip
        no matter how tantalizing faraway becomes
        wax and polish over dust and grime

While the French were fully occupied with pelts and furs
        Alsea Bay was inviolate
                filled with courtesy
                and the conventions of stillness

Though place names would come in time
        Eckman Lake
        Drift Creek
        Shepards Point
If you lived there native
        there was no need to go anywhere else

You deserve to be happy in the forest
Lost in premonition
        the uneasy ancestors in attendance

What would come to be the Crestview Golf Club
        Yaquina Bay State Park
                meaning and permanence
                like a sobriety open-ended
When you can see beyond the sea

When each day was entrusted to time
And everything you saw was reminder and myth

Have a funeral mind in America
In a western west
        that beyond which
        the world returns to old age and burial

That coast
        whose ocean sleeps above Cascadia's subduction
Sleeps until tectonics says it's time to wake Waldport

It was a magnificent isolation!
A city at the edge of an official landmass
        and it works so well
        proof a citizenry enjoys a certain mandate

To live for all time in all our places
In all our French movies remembered
        apply the nationhood of Champlain in northern rain

Oh, yes!   intellectually rigorous
You could say the drama of settlement
        was exteriority versus interiority
                people in line to move inland

The English
The Russians
        looking for an opening
                dona eis pacem
I'm going to say it's a very short story
Waldport was denouement

I long to reschedule Sir Francis Drake
                        and his Spanish counterparts
Why do I see their sails above the nearshore shanties
Right to left or left to right as opportunity affords?

We are without gold coins or silver
Yet there's enough treasure in drawing breath
        to see us safely to future seaside motels

One can say
        that a day in the fifties
                is just a next door neighbor of today
So stumble over
                borrow some sugar
                the basics

Take it easy
Let Alsea Bay be a shapeshifting mirror for the Canadian geese
        doubling their numbers with reflection
        and whatever's flying north-south

Every moment an occasion of Forever

Is it sobriety?
Yes, I think it's that
        for I would be ruining all of history otherwise
                and be remiss

Waldport is revealing itself
For as long as one can say "No!" to daiquiri
As long as thoughts come any way they hit

Archival
   that beyond
     in which the world returns
       to old imaginings
       far flung as empires

ii. Mother and Child

They will meet us northside the bridge
   with a mariner's perspective
Mother and daughter from the south
Taking turns at the wheel

Proud parent recent graduate
They will start a business
   some sideline of a sideline
     Will Smith's advance party in Waldport

Ambassadors for Sizzler
   set on acquiring new territory
Or maybe they've come for a photo shoot
     wide angle only
     black-and-white only
     portraits only

"The citizens of this little city
   they will meet us
   and we will all know what to do
     unabashed with waiting to do it

"They'll ask, 'Are you living here now?'
And they'll put us up in the little green house
   and certainly hope we stick around

"We never gave up on your coming," they'll say
"Let's have some Thai noodles
Hear you tell stories of New York
   talk all night

gaudeamus igitur!

"Going deeper, now
Don't go away
  though you're a citizen of the world
  the world can wait a little longer for you, creatures of light
Her cap and gown kept pressed
  in case the United Nations requires her services

"Meanwhile, mother
  may we make your acquaintance
   for the sake of obsession?"

It would be late afternoon at the earliest
She was keen to see Battle Rock Wayside
  and walk the streets of Port Orford
  learn the names of the galleries there

She found some pictures
Took some pictures
She even reenacted the battle with her daughter
  and it seemed a satisfactory catharsis
  though who was the Indian
   and who was the white man wasn't clear

Think they traded off until a hunger for clam chowder arose

Suffice to say they were detained by history
History and movies
  in a Port Orford inn
After all it's a holiday with all its inventory

There was thunder in the night
Thunder in search of offenders
  yet its deep bombast lulled them
  and the intermittent squalls

It was a dalliance
  yet a sensible caprice
   in lieu of no itinerary

And crossing the Alsea
  she bridges perfection with parental intellect
   the generations living poetry

And although she unlearns her own teen story
    she ensures her daughter desires more
        than Twitter's transient allegiance

The graduate approaches
    to permeate summer sameness
        with dark-robed beauty

They'll say, "How are you?"
And it will be the universe answers
    if she   the universe   answers at all

To glimpse them is pure perspective
Mother and daughter
    the hint of all the geneology you can name
        and seek in Salt Lake City
        or in the bones of the obsolete Tertiary

Bones leading not to you only
But far beyond that
    say, sixty-five million years past a bridge and a bay

iii.   Oysters

Oysters at just the right time
Oysters when the sun arrived surprisingly bright
Oysters with power to focus olfactory
Oysters a flavor as perfect as all of the sea!

The shellfish bequeathes
    says it's sorry it could not do more
        you'd eat them raw to eat them
        and suffer nausea afterwards!

There is something *usurping*
The oysters' chemistry overarching
Sea food as entity
    god of cuisine
        a specific faith

Taste for a higher palate's power

Whatever oysters are
     has brought comfort to the table
     made holes in monotony
At just the right time
        the exceptional oyster is richly psychic

You wouldn't care if it was a last meal taken

So sometime   2pm   right then
You're a free spirit
     as soon as the sunburst's arrival

Listen to the chef
He is telling us about the oyster
     and singing, "You send me…"
        the song sung to allowable heaven

Eat   then *cat*-sleep
In the middle of the day almost
     and this contentment be the plot of a daydream
     concerning life as an oyster

Made ready for butter and flame
     and the ad lib of altered circumstance

iv.   Only What I Think You Want to Hear

Only what I think you want to hear
     of the little lake
        ruffled with cold sundown air
        and the *source* of that sundown
          seen in the water brightly

Clear pooled
Or shaken roughly

Seeing   not seeing
The subject clouds forming in reflection
     till the heart of the sun is stilled with twilight

v.   **Breaking Free**

I thought breaking free should start in Waldport
As if the freedom were a marriage
        an ironic joining after determined solitude

I thought that cutting loose
        should begin right there with tying the knot
That severance a marriage
                as in "Love is Here to Stay!"

I was gone anyway
Gone away to a coast of dreams
Remembering everything
        images like friends of insight

Dress like them
        for their fabric is infused with sensibility and truth

The decks of all the ships
The shops on all the streets

Let me catch the cats of this town
        and admire their eyes after midnight
Let them follow me everywhere
                the first few days of freedom
                until I'm used to it
                        and feline as well

Feline paws and fur that will be freedom enough
And the stealth and vigilance to preserve it

Best man the mayor   if a man
The ceremony eclectic
        inclined to hippie-informal
                but pre-Summer of Love austere

And this liberation?
Let it coincide with something else
        the murmurings of faith in counterintuitive
        belief enough to trigger the rest

The western sea
                though highly symbolic

and seemingly limitless
                isn't really necessary

I wouldn't want to say it
Or that the blind are not missing something
        dearly held in painters' eyesight
                for I'm on the level
                as much as a horizon's perfectly horizontal

Lighthouses too may shutter
Close their lids
        and let philosophies shine
        engage 360 degrees of uncertainty

Even the gulls are superfluous surround sound
Surely the inner Om's the preferred oceanic Muzak
For the sake of the oh-so-elusive Peaceful Kingdom
        uncork the champagne of order
        and down it
                fizzy with presumption

It's not so long now
A turning point reached
                and mortality tamed
                the altar to which you glide

Some marriage of convenience in Waldport
And that to which you clung
        like an absent-minded scientist
        deeply concerned with forevermore's strata
                and geological promise

vi.   Still Life with Candles

Resolved to study the fruits and ceramics
The table in it
        the vase of course
                the linen's unsigned setting
                outside-shadowed

I think it is the work of random waiters
In to-and-from attendance
        tall and attentive

they've built this still life
with tips and gratuities
                    their passion in it

The table an address for casual arrangements
Some of it is purple   and luckily yellow
        yet you couldn't really say it suited a camera
        not with those eerie candles' flames

This still life's unlike others
Even the painter surrenders
        to the wick's wavering and wandering
            like amber prayers continuous
            their included paraffin

A slightly moveable feast

An array unintentioned
No patrons sit
        the fruit and bread are abandoned

What is seen
        is realtime's composition
        a movie of eyes only

And the stillness there depends on the seer
There is celery and flowers
        four peaches
            some grapes
The single apple
        as shiny as any canvas conceived by Debbie Vinograd

There might be a skull and a doll in the shadows
There could be a conch shell nestled as well

But before the brush or the lens is attempted
A decision
        a question candlelight is asking with anonymous flicker
The many tongues of evening wagging their enchantments
        disturbing the air
            that was almost still

Small fires in a little city of produce and plunder
All of it waiting in the cafe's glare

like a maitre d's altar

Stand back and study a steady state of art
As display and centerpiece
    that a busboy contrived
        between tables cleared for compost

Let its elegant garbage attest
    to a disposal that masquerades as minimalist buffet

The candles count the years so far
Of a business sense
    half a dozen senses
    no, eight!
        Infinity's flames

It is acumen derived from a salt sea awareness
And what will work
    that's fulltime fulfillment

Hoffmann's cinematic orgy-banquet in Venice
    what the revelers left and self-denied

Be still!
Be still
    and be sufficiently organic
        embellished with flame
        in the aftermath of dinner and dance

Eat without talking in Mystery's public places
Talk without eating
    glow without oxygen
        wick-attached paraffin seraphim
Long distance close-up and quivering

In Waldport apartments   precious spaces
    evacuated

vii.   Splash Zone

Where the sea's apron is flung
And under-the-sea is briefest
    and the opposite of a tsunami's super flood

Splash zone
Tentacles
        furthest reach of the ninth ninth wave

The button barnacles survive the ultraviolet
The no-name tread is fine friction for a shoe

Just enough of the Pacific
        to settle the issue of life and death
                in favor of the former

The tide's fingers spread like a laying on of hands
        and the rocks blossom
It is meager sanctuary
                that tells of white lie survival
                        flung

viii.   Party Boat Blues

The new yacht is a slum afloat
Everyone's angry
        a seasick coterie
                you'd think it was the mafia, Miami
The tax attorney scared he won't survive the seagoing sitdown

"I hate to say it, Mugsy
        but the Feds aren't going away any time soon!"

Clink!   they're sloshed
Someone's retching at the stern
And there's the Coast Guard
        the glint of binoculars raised

"Whaddya doin' wid da helm?   Jesus H!"
"Hey, you sure you're not Donnie Brasco, my friend?
"Linda!   more ice!"

You've heard of "in the wrong hands," right?
Well, they enjoy the party while they can
The boat's been stolen
        hustled
                commandeered

It would take Thomas Jefferson's marines to recover it
And these pirates
     are lawyered up
     liquored up
        paranoid curmudgeons

"Hey!   you're spilling your drink into the fish tank!"
"So you wanna' sail to Shanghai?
     you don't even have charts!
        what an amateur
You'd get as far as the end of the pier and run aground!"

"Shoulda' bought my cousin's catamaran
Better for getaways   runaways
Like *you*, honey!
    oh, don't be mad I said that
       come back
       come here
          I meant nothin'

"Hey, Paul!   get a load of that seagull!"

"Yeah, he's the only one having fun around here!"

Clink!   the banquet
Clink!   indigestion
Clink!   whoops!   the captain's gone overboard!

"Hey, the captain fell in!
We *need* him!   dive in!"

The music's mostly eighties schlock
A retro trance
     the boss is being sentimental
     his territory
        his taste
          his broads

Don't insult the host
You dance   you dance drunk
    as if at a wedding party of frayed relatives
A gangster happening suffused with blues
    at anchor and bobbing

No movie stars can save the script
            clipped
            mechanical
                  like the printing of money

I remember a woman named Esther
She once said that dollars were frog skins
      and she didn't care if they flowed her way

Where are you now, Esther of Berkeley?
Are you still enlightened in that faraway bay?

What's afloat on this one's unsavory unseaworthy
Would that sobriety might take the helm
      and take away their waiting
          for the party's a progression from bad to worse

The dolphin tries to mind amends the strife
Discord taught to stand by
      and let frolic return and drift with the tide
          change the tune a little
But the mob is not secure in their boat
Believes their fortune is finite

Antique voices sound in the sea breeze
And ancient monsters are apprised of fresh opportunities
      for extortion and fraud

The genius of crime heard in "All aboard!"
And a life energy fueled by alcohol

Does the party have a purpose?
"Hey!   Luigi, my friend!   who's dealin'?"
"How about Canasta instead?
      in the old days we'd play Canasta…"
"You're wanting a game of Canasta?"
"Canasta."
"What the hell's Canasta?"
"I'll teach ya'   it's a great card game
Look!   we can't do anything until the principals arrive
      and it will take your mind off our troubles"

"Hey, Poker will do!"

You'd think it was the mafia
It *was* the mafia
        with a veneer of decency
            the boat afloat
                    innocuous
                    monied
Of the Waldport inventory of play things
Pertaining to regata, sunscreen and vodka

Ambition's boat
Bought and paid for
                        with impatience
                        irascibility
                        libido and pride
In short   all the values held by a playground bully

The assurance
        that with enough intimidation
            one's aggression
                may be mistaken for smarts
                    capable of exciting a professor

One that's meek and over-specialized
Red-tortured   tenured   and unfulfilled

The yacht means drugs again
They need to make a decision
It's business   a business decision
They are used to informality
        and the liberal use of slang
        slang to the point of mutual incomprehension

Below deck it's "Hushaby!"   "Shh!"
The boss's wife:

"Hushaby, baby
You the man!   make it happen!   you know
You said you'd take care of me
        all right   it's cool   you the man
            come over here!
            you want me to do all the talkin'?

"You want me?   then do the lovin'

You want me to sit down with you
        when you have the sitdown?

"Hey, baby!   make me a drinky, okay?
Make it 'sex on the beach,' please
        and then
        pretty-please-with-sugar-on-top
            make me happy, honey!

"C'mon!
You'll be able to think right after that
        so have a dose of me, baby!
Be an animal!   be that animal, big boy!
Forget we're married
        I'm that hooker, okay?
Watcha' gonna do, huh?
                        that's right!
                        that's better!

"Hey, 'Heart of Glass,' remember?
'Donnie Brasco,' remember?
        'Heart of Glass'"

"That'll work   yeah, sweetheart!
I remember and you're beautiful
Love the one you're with, baby
        and I'm with youse!   Mmmmmmmm!"

Well, it was decision time
        and it was getting late and later
        later on
And no one wanted to dump the body in the bay

The boy
        while guilty of squealing
                was still very much a beloved boy
And for old times' sake the gang was conflicted

They just wished their collective problem hadn't happened
Wished they could have partied without a conscience
But the party assuaged the deed
        and they tried to relax and forget

The crux of the matter at hand

And about to go down
    like a ship to the bottom
        the here and now oppressed

Besides the unlucky boy
    someone *else* had overstepped
    someone busted someone's balls

"Sit down
I said *siddown*!!
That's what you do at a sit down
Okay   present and accounted for

"Jimmy, you disappoint me
Shut *up* when I'm talkin' to youse!
What?   you're seasick?
    well I'm seasick of *you*
      sea-sick-and-tired
        and depending on your answers to my questions…

"We're all going to decide what's next
Ya got dat?   *Good!"*

There were a lot of pissed off gangsters on the boat
But a mourning also
    for Anthony had been a very good boy

ix. Gauguin's Bathers Remained

Though it's cold outside
Though the tide has collapsed
    and is telling lies about summer
      and even the clams
      are inclined to quit the sea
        and keep to their shells on land

Though a strange sheen has appeared
    and the sea's surface is unruffled
    and the sun shining black above

Though the waves have stopped
    and made a bath of the Pacific
      silent

no longer battering its headlands

Gauguin   in his wisdom
        has placed his nudes reclining
                right here
                and seeming nescient
                        of aught but the artist's presence

TOLOVANA PARK

If you buy here
    closer you could not live to the rocks
        Haystack Rock
        and The Needles

If you move in
    closer you could not be to the boulder field
        and its nightmare barnacles

Closer to blank secrecy's dens
    and the mysteries of rockfall you could not be
        and still be warmed by a fireplace

"Tolovana," the Indian syllables say
To privilege
    to empire
        and frontier's finish
        just a hundred yards away
           two *minutes* away

Make it a winter's day you go
When you go
    entering the spectacle
    that's a backyard seascape
What death would be
        on the rocks
        punctual

One operates a share of phantasmagoria
Reality kissed by its opposite
Reality *deviant*
    weightless   Planet Tolovana

The Extra Vehicular Activity is outside the house
    in the alien theater
        whose wordplay is a recital of puns
It is *so* relaxing!

And being this close to the monolith
    hide away in its shadow
        unspoiled creature of delight

The future a certainty qualified by words

You're married to the shore   unhurriedly
It is the kind of love
        that kinks time such
                you can say eternity passed
                and it was just a day

Just a day down which the void abyss descended
        and opened the clocks
        for suspense and belonging
                belief and sequester

Your neighbors obey the same gods as yourself
Druids
        and they consider the seastacks Stonehenge
                that journeyed from England
                and shapeshifted

Tolovana   potential   mechanism
That which calibrates alarm
        all anxiety
        the ocean floor's crushing pressure
All the people
                who have ever imagined danger for your benefit

Do I live in the house?
Or amateurishly sit
        za-zen after a fashion
                in the zen garden's seaweeded rocks
At one with squish and squirt
And the sudden inundation of a ninth ninth wave?

There's a law breaking down
A law which prefers mystery to justice
There seems no equality in Tolovana
        and the misfortunes of shellfish continue
        the menace of the drilling radula horrifying!

Please pray on!
        that vicious oceanography
                not too much intrude our contemplations

Safe enough

Safe enough
    age well
    age well enough in Tolovana
Like money from home spent on a last depression

You *will* get drunk
And you *will* get arrested

No, no   it's all right
Shake your head
    disbelief you live in tidy ruins
        live interior pantomimes

An inside
Unpaid
    except for a sense of privilege
      water-content
      soul
      abeyance
        real estate

As this is the genie's wish to remove himself from the bottle
He takes into account the humans were self-absorbed
    but their wishes became a weariness
No one knows his hiding place
    so they'll have to make it happen without him

A clean break!
Free as the rain that falls
    on his brand new bottle of incidental truth
Divorced too from the Middle East
      and all its expectations

He'll spend the first new hours in decompression
He's crashing
And I'm crashing
    his pad
      as alter ego brat genie
      just a shadow until the town is lost

He said not to waste time   and I haven't
I bring him along at low tide
    teach him the names of the starfish
    their Latin like an ancient pentecostal improv

with rock-written eastern spells

Tolovana quiet
Except for the children
        and new construction

It is as if those who remember the Age of Eisenhower
        guess the hour of its ending

The winters attempt to instill an energy
And their gales are welcome
        as sober notions and resolve

Yet the jury is out
And the residents
        reluctant to forsake their melancholy

RETURN TO THE TOWN CALLED CANARY

What canary sang?
And was it yellow?
What year?
What paintbrush moved?

And who moved the paintbrush and colored the house
        the *only* house?

There's a railcar cottage there
        where you study the river's strengths and weaknesses
The cold parallels laid down
        like a split virtue
                involuntarily steely
                slowly becoming aware

Yellow not needing to explain anything

Yellow shining in the rainy day
        suddenly canary
And gray is disgraced for having taken to depression

You should know
        the valley's mostly historical never-never
A pacification plan supervised by a bird
                whose first name I long to learn

When the night comes will the lights go on?
Or will the remainders of the town be dark
        a landscape's single-minded blur?

Well, it's all we needed anyway
Who we are that are impoverished

Entered the circle
The little map's circle of a town called "Canary"
Entered   a stranger to its long days' hours

From the west I came
        full of crimes you'll never know
                unless you let me love you
                like a catholic mission to do so

The visit will be hands-on   hands extended
As if it were the Brahms D Minor piano concerto
So play it   especially the trills
        the historic trills

Come to Canary
        and sit on the pavement
                in a *recital* of trills
There are no graffiti visible
This is what it's like to be a ghost
        and *specifically* a phantom from Canary

There is yellow multiplicity
Photographs try to enclose it
        the land within that enclosure
        the drooping stalks of a yellow flower's folds
An alternative energy shining in its botany's bulbs

I'm the only citizen as such
        and live in a car
                the twenty seconds it takes
                to enter and leave the little town

Brief residence in this retirement of hours spent
Moving backwards in time
        to perform a concert of research

Where you live is where you *are*
        and wait   in the town's profundity
        drawn forth from the single word of itself
Canary never known
American Canary in a day more pale than most
        low ceiling's gravitas

We're going to be little forever with the help of a spaniel
There should be a farmhouse to help with this
There *should*
        for this is as far as we go today on the arterial
                a bird as destination
                bird as still life geometric
                                a lyric construction

An island town not a poem

Not a poem at all

What's in that house, though?
What stove
        rafters
                drawers and beds?
Whose names have been said and whose left unmentioned?
Was their first phone made   two-part?
Whose shoulder tapped and footsteps heard?

Canary's inland   didn't work out
It was *supposed* to but it didn't
        though it stood on tiptoe to do so and stare at the stars

There's an obvious bend in the river
Where's the ocean now you're gone?
                can someone come out and play?

Blues   and yellows in the blues
Surely *someone* kept a journal
        of the days and nights
                that Canary sang a song of the Coast Range
Broke the spell of the wind and the rain
Broke the spell of "got the news"

There was a side of Canary
        that eschewed the forest monsters
        and terraformed the valley
And was songful
                like canaries' nothing-to-it
                nothing-at-all

ORICK

i. The Theater

You could go into an imaginary theater
  for such is Orick's somehow

You could enter into agreement
The doors could open
And with that unlocking
  it could be said
    that Orick's Orick Theater was open again

If only briefly

Its double marquee
  and twice-spelled name
    once more meaningful

Of course there's no time for a screening
Unless
  unless
    well, there *would* be time
    if the owner saw fit
        now, *wouldn't* there?

Some persuasion!
Negotiating!
And who knows?
  the needed steps might be taken
    a projector found
      and quickly installed
      to throw a movie on the screen

A small audience content
  with their bucket of buttered popcorn popped
A single batch for a one-time show

It is a pale dull green building otherwise
Peaceful apartments opposite
  the haven of La Hacienda
  serving one's heart's desire for Mexican fare
    six years to the day

after its penurious grand opening

See what may be started
And finished
on a gray-green day in a small town

If you enter
will it be a Bogart?
a silent?
Or a nineteenth century trip to the moon
that whirrs and purrs in the Orick revived?

Think it over
while a contrary bird
goes against the onshore air
and seems to hover over 101's coastal path

Passing the theater
with as much reluctance as myself

ii.   The Orick Cow

There was a certain slow-motion cow in progress
Fence post to fence post
and sporting black splotches

They'd left her out there
not so *very* far away
not so far away at all

"Where'd they go, by the way?

"Never mind   I'm here, cow
And if you want
I'll milk you if you need some milking
It would be no trouble but you'd have to coach
It's been sixty years since my last attempt!"

It is a solitary beast
without cunning or too much ambition
And nodding her head
beyond the fence
in her very green backyard acre of pasture

Trying to find that favorite spot, maybe

"Would you let me pet you?
Would you let me into your life today
        and that way help me be a good citizen of Orick?

"I feel like coming home to a place
To lie awake in the dark the first night, probably
Where will I go otherwise, cow?

"All is black-and-white like you
A black-and-white question

"But I guess I'm not ready, darling bovine"

She prances and nods her head
And then
        munching grass
                in the tsunami hazard zone
                        she asks a question of her own:

"Can you get me the hell out of here?"

iii.   The Gift Shop

I'd mention your name if I dare
Owner   proprietor
        and say you have a retinue of carvers
        busily engaged
                say, for thirty years

And you'd planned it that way   gloriously!

Yes, your name may yet be told
Though what a *name* could add
        to your entrepreneurial accomplishments
                is not at all clear

To say a name is advertisement
And it is not my purpose
        to propose anyone should buy your wood
Well, they *should* of course

But rather
    I'd evoke a sense of what's required to sculpt it
What eschewing of other distractions
    in order to concentrate on *this* work!

For instance, the mirror
Told as three thousand dollars of glass
    surrounded by a redwood frieze
    detailed as *any* relief one may imagine

Had I gone crazy in the dark myself
    such a piece may have occurred to me
        demanding it be done
Mirror in the middle   surrounded by sculpture
Where one's *reflection* would be of little interest

The mirror was one of many

You'd named the woods
There was of course the myrtle
    in all of its complexions
        the main reason I'd entered the store

I'd thought to latch onto a cheaper bowl
In order to show its color and grain
    to a friend
    in the southern distant town of Palo Alto
The present to have a rock supplement
    gotten from the Samuel Boardman corridor

Thought to get a myrtle sample
And I stayed to study your store
    and take   with permission
        picture after picture

There was something maple, you said
    and drew attention
    to the darkness of its being!

It was the kind of place   where
    the longer you stayed
        the more amazement climbed its stairs
So that the day's agenda is then revised
            or even forgotten

The various to-dos calmed to unhurried possibilities
And *sculpture* mind
    carver mind
        are thoroughly awakened

Oh!   native woods!
The word "xyloid" forming in one's speech
    with its "z" sound said

There were buckeye examples
The buckeye and all its tendencies and properties
    known to you and your helpers

And the polishing?
Making smooth the splinters?
I could apprentice be to that
    and be happy a metaphor was found
        to assuage the hurts
           of rough
           and approximate living

The buckeye crazy with fungus
And modification
    the almost lunatic colors coming online the brain
    as if the mind had always desired them
        and dared to resonate their wishes

I've been always arriving
And those arrivals outweighed a motive to depart
Four   and counting   walls
    of far more than planar enclosure

The point-and-shoot
    has barely begun to capture the shiny inventory
And with its wide-angle reconnoitering
    the lens is crowded with multiplicity's knick-knacks

I might mention your name
I *will*!   Robert Coombs!
    and you're casual
        talking easily with Germans
          who've perhaps come all the way from Heidelberg
            to handle redwood

        and return to Europe
    post-haste

I wish Mister Coombs had a radio show
A chance to expand!
He'd make a fine *film*   all by himself
    validation
    and young for his age
Profound in the sense he's open to change

Open as the ocean
    the creek called "Redwood"
        the early bird that empties the sky
        every stone turning slowly

The gift shop was begun some year of the eighties
Being a *specific* enterprise
    when all the works within it belie limitation

As though each seed of inspiration
    were a portal to worlds within worlds
All that carving
        coming closer to accomplishment
          than a carnival's worth of sideshows
Or the only *approximate* satisfaction
    of doing it *all*
    and especially all at *once*

It must have seemed strange starting up
A transition not wholly expected
Perhaps you might have felt
    you'd reneged on a larger opus

But now it seems a trusted universe
    burgeoning detail
    your slivers all attended
And oh!   the creatures formed!
        or had formed *for* you!

What a wooden menagerie in place
Not even to be disturbed by any purchase

My animal self knows uncommon restraint
Walking the aisles

without dislodging or tipping
      and no sudden reflex or elbows
Like enhanced propriety and best behavior

Mister Coombs, there's a woman
A woman up north in Reedsport
    and she too has a store
      one more of many more

And it was *her* business brought me to yours
The first captivation was her shelves of myrtle
And after that
    the eye stayed true
      and sought the same art elsewhere

Your name is known but hers is forgotten
The workmanship
    has made me mad to capture the skill
      if only in the throwaway sense
      disposable as art divorced from reputation

Robert Coombs!   counselor!
I've brought pralines and other refreshments
You'll talk me down
    from a steady state of anger
    oh!   and free-floating envy

Nothing got done
    that could compare
      with these variations on a *theme* of wood
But only a porch is attained
The prospect of apprenticeship too great a bewilderment

You'll make it better   the great work is done
And a craft established
    what was in the tree revealed
      all this in the trees!
      I'll walk among them
        walking the forest!

A gift shop *prior*
Artifacts enclosed in the bark
    that long for human hands
    and how *good* hands borrow

As if those hands
        would transmute
        without harm done
                this height above the forest floor

Merciful hands!
        that navigate the grains' white lines
            as keepsake lumber
When you walk all day in choosing

A sideline lining up with the main
        to be intoxicating measure
        and occasion

Just that *mirror* take and take seriously
Made intricate yourself with looking

The same story told
        that varies so subtly
            a lifetime's reflected
            always mysterious
Mirror in the middle
                the carving a commentary
                thick-framing

And every *objet* is *trouve*
Found   and found to be repented?
        thematic
            and hard to choose out of so many

If the art is handled it cannot be put back
For they are the counterparts to hypnoglyphs
        hand-held
        commanding
        tempting
            inviting stealage and lawlessness!

I see my own arrest
For being a slacker
                an outsider
                a dilettante
                    and poser

Yet   in acquiring the wood
      may I find employment sufficient
              to stave off a reckoning
Distant San Francisco unreturned to
The City just an evocation

There is no other Other
And so retreat
      into the complimentary familiar
         you'd thought to be strange

The expertise in carving
The visualization that attends
Be an agency of one exile only
      with escape velocity
         leaving Planet Cement
        and all its mansions
                tilting

iv.   The Surge

When the earthquake came and the wave began
      you knew it was a wave that would go every which way
      and everywhere it knew it could
On its way to whatever shore it wanted
With Japan the start   the beginning

It was the kind of wave that disappeared in deep water
You'd never be able to measure its height
      so slight
         was the oscillation then

Only the shores could bring it to life
Only the beaches
      the coves
         the bays and estuaries
Only the *edges* of the ocean

And it was not known
      the amplitude
         the run-up
            the *surge*
               the extent of it

All of this was so very much a guess

But it's always all day and all night
Advance and retreat
        advance and retreat
                until the energy's gone

And you can *watch* all day and night
                the wave
                that is always sloshing slow-motioning
                        in the hideouts of all the Pacific
                                Orick, even

Where Redwood Creek   is for a while
Just dangerous enough to draw a crowd to the bridge
        to see height above normal

Just as at Brookings
        Crescent City and Santa Cruz
                the wave
                that was many
                        frighteningly entertained
And tried to make the creek run backwards

Orick!
An assault
        that was a Midway
                a Dutch Harbor
                        Attu and Kiska
                                Wake and New Guinea
                                        The Philippines
                                                Hawaii
All the samurai become a force of nature!

What was sought in Hirohito's palace
Perfected and found to be neutral destruction
        devoid of imperial ambition

The wave
        without the blare of "The Pacific March"
                to make it fearsome

As though the tsunami
        for all its power to terrorize

         lacked the will to succeed
And was   therefore   inexplicably and strangely
    benign

v.   Orange and Yellow

It is a story of orange and yellow told
Of gas and more
       south side of Orick
The Necco wafer station-store

Orange letters on a yellow background

"Got gas?   got gas?
Well, you can have some of ours
     like a bee arriving a colorful flower
Fill up with our nectar flammable
You can see from the sign we could explode!"

This is an establishment
     that loves the colors orange and yellow
A two-part pastel outpost
      as many ways asserting orange and yellow
         as the Shoreline Market
        with all those potted
               slanted
               plants on display

A business
A story starting fresh as the onshore morning
     middle and end of it
        opposite the adorable cow
        and its black-and-white movie
Silent almost

Yester town on the river's floodplain

Gotta let go and get a guitar
And song-write the service station
     like a phantom memory
     forever believing
        there must be a home heart to inhabit

Orange lost and yellow found
Cast a spell   painting and repainting
Can you see light shining?
        can you?
                the two colors' claim to recognition

A search could end here   or just begin
Orick as depot of light between green and red

A primary yellow and secondary orange
Scheme like a proposition
        that citrus holds sway
                in the acidic sense
And vitamin C is a splish-splash affair

Let go and learn some chords!
You could entertain the customers
                come to the Shoreline Market
Get them all home
        in time for a din-din
                derived from its seaside produce

You are not to ever worry the town's too small
        and everyone will know your business
At least the town will be taking an interest in you
And isn't that what you wanted all along?

That someone might do
Do and make you a project   a local
        but famous
        in the sense
                that Orick is a small enough town for such things

MANILA

i.   Manila's What You Come To

Manila's what you come to
        right turning your way on highway 255

Manila expressed as certain houses
An appraisal
        driving past houses others own

There's a dark blue house with a garage
        that seems the opposite of hysteria
                the basketball net prepared for a game of HORSE

The door is light green
I want to enter   make an excuse
        and see if Philippine tagalog is spoken
                say it's a survey
                a freelance poll

There are pale blue slats about the dark blue house
And a West Coast fence ideally placed
        and thrillingly maintained

Manila has power
All the power they want
        for there are power lines beyond the blue
        and they slightly droop with suspension
                scissoring
                dividing
                        and making the sky line
                        powerful

Let me be electrocuted
I'm willing to grasp the learning

Note a second house more modern
Unless the available light is trickster
        it's gray-blue
                with a decided peak
                        wide windows and a skylight

Anyone in the world may live there
Let us congratulate them

But wait, there's more   a light pink house
And on the other side the road
        beyond the cypress
                there's a woodpile
                with spiders probably

There's a chainlink
Lupin Avenue
        the street sign a telltale alluding to flowers

Where are we going
        so fast we'd have missed it?
A quick visit to the Philippines
                in search of a capitol city of same
                some ultimate authority
Anything to control my unruly American heart

I'm catholic in the dunes
And trying to hypnotize the locals
        happy in the role
                a different house each day
Starting with dark blue

Applying spiritual principles
Keeping it simple
        as little bells heard
        or chimes in the onshore

Higher power dunes
Higher power winds
            and a busy body/mind
They'll have to throw me out of here

But I've come for the tsunamis too
Their irresistible physics!
        the entrancement of a rising ocean
        and its multiplication tables
The houses others own
            owned by the sea

Holdfast dwellings

Profoundly   holistically   drowned
        the old cars parked and flooding

How mysterious it is
        to contemplate breakdown and rust
So far Manila's obscure
Known only to paintbrushes

But there *might* be a reason for potentates to come
For presidents and sheikhs to show up
Something might possess them
        to make their own appraisal
        play a little basketball in a very small court

Maybe HORSE
The random locations
        from which a basket may be made to swish
With practice they'd never miss

Manila   capitol   secure
        and only modestly consuming

Be careful what you pray for
The whole story told
        it may turn out
                the best love in the world took place right here

In a blue house or pink
Before anyone thought to avoid it
Before Planned Parenthood
        and after nunnery vows and "How come?"

Well, that's unknown in the wind and the rain
Just wanted to know if you deserve it
                and you do
The weather's fine
        the power lines buzz
                and so far no one's objected to a tourist or two

ii.   The Humboldt Coastal Nature Center

The Humboldt Coastal Nature Center
"Friends of the Dunes"

Friends well met and full of purpose
Who've joined to say, "Hiking, no camping"
        and that's okay
        really it is

There's a strange construction
Like a section of subway
A tunnel through a very large dune
        ah!   an artificial rise
                it is part of whatever the hole is part of

The orange plastic an explicit advisory

"Stay out while we make it
        rain or shine
                keep away
                        men working
                                breaking
                                        lunching"

It is a bore of a few yards only   a portal
What could it possibly be
        that takes shape in a dark day of raindrops?
How's it going?

What could it possibly be
                with a house on top
                if that is what it is?

Then there's a long, low ancient barn nearby
Chock full of extraneous
A radio plays
        the barn door swung open for inspection
There's an overturned plastic chair and an outhouse

Whatever it means it's meant to be private
Private property
        ownership's shabby alliteration
                wanting a break from language

Put two-and-two together now
Don't be dense
The construction's related to the prose of the sign

and it matter-of-factly announces
all you need to know of the tunnel

Surely I will connect the two
And go henceforth informed
                              lively, even

Let's look again into the barn
It just may be someone's shaved by now
        and is ready to greet dumbstruck strangers
        who are slow to grasp things
                and outsmile the ducks there are

Good!   no one showed
My imbecility saved for sealife later
        when I'll keep a *diary* of my foolishness
        and try not to let on I was ever human

Right now
        take the trail under the power lines
                take the trail away
                as if you were a downed flier in occupied France
                        and need to be circumspect
                        furtive

Get your bearings and begone
Down the winding way to the beach
        between sharp blackberry briars
        and what is like that
                seizing available space
                with full botanical expression

The purlieu   related land
And what did the broadside say and imply?
        "Go back!   it's important!
        Alexander's coming   or came!"

A beach ball featuring ukuleles
        Jessicurl
                special guests from the Arcata Theater's lounge
All of this imagined in Manila's dunes
Ma-le'l Dunes North Unit

Humboldt Coastal Nature Center

Say it!   just the sound of the words overjoys!
That's what's being built
A work in progress
        as I am in progress
        to Arcata over there
        in the hybrid landscape
                believing in oeillades
                and books made from movies of Manila

Believing a bunch of potholes
        on a muddy track
                will get you to the tunnel
Just craters in the rain

GREEN NEPTUNE

It was very green
Greener than anything anywhere else

It just so happened
    like an insight made visible
At the last stop before the run to Eureka south

Neptune   the unfamiliar   mystic emerald
Something gave it green
All the green you need
    all its phases
    as if the color had been flung there
           draped year by year

Made a better afternoon than all the rest of the rainbow's cloth
The oldest shore we'd seen so far
    yet it sprang into equinox as if for the first time

A Christmas green
And all the inhabitants of Christmas carols
    now and suddenly
        Greensleeves of the sea

Having seen it in the afternoon
    it should be always afternoon it's seen
There better be a sun
Because a sun had made the green a success
    beyond money's pale powers to attract
        something crazy like that

I have a witness   James
And we have photos
    in support of a theory of Neptune that ends in green

Imagine heaven
    as having at least a little of these shades of green

It was as if Glenn Ingersoll had happened by
    and painted the same as he *wrote* about green
That writing copied and given away

We don't exaggerate!
It was a View-Master's view we entered
    and we photoshopped its fringes
        the many edges inviting

Although there were no jobs to be had
    you could still appreciate the situation
        be Neptune's apprentice
Shipwrecked sailors squandering time and time again green
Though trying not to be partisan

Didn't know that Oz had a seashore
    way west of the Winged Monkeys
    and their colorless castle

If you crash a car and can't go on
And Triple A comes and *they* can't go on
    there's enough color green lying around
        to requite the lost love of an engine

Having an Irish marriage in Neptune's chapel
    is exchanging rings without changing continents

The coast is definitely wearing the green
Be kind to its mermaids
    singing "Green Grow the Lilacs" to landlubber Eliot

Take 'em home and have a harem, T.S.!
Be a god of all this   like Neptune
You changed society
    now change your life!

It may be "The Night of the Living Day"
And we're all working graveyard
    by the light of illumined emeralds
        but we don't want the news to cover it
Any of it!
Not these Christmas apparitions

They'd just get it wrong
And bring crowds that would *also* get it wrong

Neptune Beach is the middle lane removed
    from the highway north-south

       shuttling hues
       and serious about it

And the pleasures found on its green-sunglassed shore
     are less than half the price
          of a holiday eggnog constructed by Doctor Seuss

It's offline as much as disconnected may be
     and still be a part of the known universe

Don't touch!
It's a better painting than all of the Louvre

And the beach is something heard long distance
Like Holtz's mystic sopranos
     the last planet whirling blue-green away

Even during the Great Depression
     Neptune Beach must have looked like this
     as it looked beyond all economies and bankruptcies

There's a fence   rough-hewn
It refers to drop-off
     but *gently*
        a more rustic warning
Part of a perfect symbiosis
Part of a set

What opera does it help?
What matinee
     that uses this sun's nearly level light?
Perhaps a green extravaganza of Scriabin
        who loved to have color with his music

He went so far he went to India   almost
Bought a sun helmet ahead of time

Take him for a walk on Cummins Ridge
That his fever may abate somewhat
That he may conduct in his sleep

Don't even bring your Nikon here
     for you are not separate from the picture

Green Tara's behind it   this Indian green
    the entire forest a path
        come closer!
        do you see this?

It is a post-prison green
An emerald buddha beginning a ceremony
    and we're just in time for the procession
It seems that having once happened
    it *always* is happening
    thousands of times

This is Neptune's documentary sonata
           in a demonstration garden
A marine garden come ashore
      and having no restrictions

If Captain Cook ever landed here
    nearby   near to Neptune
Perhaps he entered the greenhouse too
Discovered Neptune's genius
      and rehearsed for Hawaii among these evergreens

The future's uncreated
The captain's short-term stays extended
    and he has time for Ten Mile Ridge
He's offline as ourselves
        late afternoon

And the cyclops Polyphemus
    son of Neptune
      keeps an eye out for us

Needless to say, it's very green right now
Green as anything
    it just so happens   mystic emerald
Like an insight
      that made for a better afternoon than ever before

With Carols calling other Carols
Now   and suddenly

SHORE ACRES REHEARSAL

He had to find a secluded place for the speech
It was an *important* speech and it had to go well
Had to be Shore Acres
      the garden by the sea

He beat the panic   beat the heat
Obama kept his words out of earshot
His address would be Exhibit A
      among the flowers and the rest of the garden

Thinking a The Rose Garden West was just right
Thinking of the things he'd say
      he opened then the origami
         acceptance like the flowers'!

A noble black man lives in the White House
No more may skin be a factor
      and he might channel all of Africa

He's going to leave the miasma
He's going to the moon
Going to get better now
      switching to the *present* tense

There's plenty of room for him to rehearse
It was a lie to have said any otherwise
He went all the way west to get straight with the east

Went to a seaside garden
      to say such things as needed to be said
         and they'll *all* be surprised!
         with a balance obtained

He will not be a victim of history
There are ghosts all waiting
      to hear his recital
         Frederick Douglass
         Booker T.
         W. E. B. Du Bois
               oh, yes
And Marian Anderson's *especially* happy and sings!

So that's it   no excuses   no blame game

"No more divided shall we be after this!
The rehearsal's assured
      and this is what I'll damned well say!"

CANNON BEACH

Most precious sea!
Previous sea!

And lonely such
        that emperors adjourn their courts
                and kings contract their kingdoms
                    to have their solitude's toes in the brine

Reimagine adolescence
Youth encompassed
        to pursue a single cannon

Turns out Shangri-La was a sea level town
Encrusted with endless days and nights

Start to say it
        the history
            what the unhurried chronicles aver
The ocean and the boy
                watching each other
                wondering what each would do

The shapeshifting tide   whimsy's child
No right path
Everything we had together
        starts with a curve in the road
        when you see it

Haystack Rock an exhibit
In a different country than ever before
What back to school should be
                        and be well-*wanted*

A teenage sea with monolithic lava
        and just for the hell of it   1957
        in the center of the century
                                    almost
I'd go begging for it all over again

There were so many dreams that whirled away from it
And I took a chance on the subconscious

place and time having run away

But here is still time to find flowers
        before the Valentine's Day of death should dawn

Cannon Beach be a gate
The ultimate western
        with villains run out of town
                to wade among the nearshore jellyfish
                and be stung by circumstance
Surely the Audubon book knows which animals

Pretend it's a man o' war   a Portuguese
Not a jelly but a siphonophore

Pretend the rocks belong to Altair 4
        the planet
        the movie
Age thirteen you're allowed
It isn't grownup world   *oh*, no!
                not yet
                not here
                        it's uncreated

I rejoiced in the cold, cold currents
Where they go in the near-shore sea
        down streets of a basalt city of Miocene stone

Consider the tide walks back across its low damp Sahara
The mind covers and uncovers
        and the heart of introductions said
                there are dreams that may now be told
We are so safely beyond any possible consequences

The coast and its screaming gulls win
And morning is found in a camera's glance
        is studied up on
                reviewed over and over
Until the Haystack's fixed features are glossy with discovery

Morning before your piano teacher's up
So early   even the locals still dream in a prelude to coffee

It's the twelfth year since World War Two

Let black-and-white be the photographs accordingly

The Japanese never made it this far
They fell short of the Land of the Clatsop
But *we did* show up
Students and teacher
        breaking the law for a little trespass
                having crossed over the Columbia

Even August can be cold enough to start a religion
All night the breakers' multi-voiced stereo
Tide out
        tide in
                the office of sleep is held

Cannon Beach was the first Away that really counted
When the virgin mind
        ran on a schedule of enthrallment
        and mainstream magic

Praise the cold, cold sea
                        and filament sky
Beach like a boulevard wide as Arabia!
I saw The Third Man walking on it
        all the way to Lion Rock
He said he'd tried to stay in his movie

I'd said I understood
And would have stayed myself
            in this *Forbidden Planet* place
Its distance away is like ending itself
By the side of the road expanded

What's in the castle?
Castle Rock is not so far   south you see it
        a blue day's journey by canoe

I want to show you Audubon's playground
Starting with the seawall
        Ecola Inn's concrete prow
        ready for another 1938's season of storms
                and Christian guitars

But Jesus forgot to love these shores

Made it hard to get back to the garden
        though we're not sad about that
Better The Needles stand dark and stark
            and not a little forlorn
            like something unfound by anyone

You will acquire these tax-deductible treasures
The locals say there was a third Needle spire
        that rose some century before
            a beaten down remembrance
            rogue waves in the story
                    really?

And certainly there's candidate rubble
Nearly submerged
        almost never seen
                barely platforms
Visible and brought to attention by minus tides

And when they turn
        after idling the seabed
It is always a remarkable flood
Loving every minute of the moon's long-distance love

Cannon Beach
A village asleep in the late millennium
        the Blue Gull Inn   candlelit
                built to suit traveling teens
                a *staging* motel

This is sharing a secret with you
Like a financial advisor
        where treasure's concerned
        where a cannon came ashore
                as part of the deck of a wreck

A new dictionary's needed   large print
And catering to all things coastal
For the city mind misspells the country's
        one thousand new words
                the better to say what dreams
                what *college* of dreams
                    dreamt in the middle of the day

Stoic contrast   tired feet
And fear of heights
        on the moistened shales
        en route to some bird's nest
An ecology barely nestled

Take me up to that place
The volcanic crevice
        zone of falling rock   igneous
                to an adult version of danger

Where's your hard hat?
Your balance for the shock wave of the west wind?

"Don't want to go home," I said
        and so I didn't and *said* I did
        dreamed I did
First time   the teacher was in it
Driving me again
        to a bluff that doesn't exist in the waking state

And there we had ourselves a look around
A darkened strand it was
        but we had night vision
The overview required
As if it were a future to be read like a palm

And I did not take my hand away
        until I'd counted the tsunamis to come
It was the first time for the unconscious
Shrouded dancers seen
                the entire thing an overture

Please don't cry!   it's only the heart
That surrender
        so drink deeply
                for we had nearly lost the cannon's solitary artillery

I always believed I'd hear it
In sunlight or darkness
                in the night of seagulls

Dream that's like a legend concerning teacher and student
As though what he said was something to live for

A philosophy of music proposed with gestures

The wreckage of Haystack Rock
        capes south and north
                and Tillamook Lighthouse
                with one month of manned lighthouse to go!

The automatic fiery future would take it from there
And be true to itself in turn

The dim headlands backgrounded a lecture and instruction
                the teacher all-inclusive
There was ghetto in the offing
        and amazement came and went like the night wind
        while he warned me away from crime's nightmares

He'd brought a compass
        to confirm it was a western sea we saw
                and his speech was one great "Hearken!"

I thought I should listen carefully indeed
As in music   when you play and play well

I'd join the honor society of leap year babies
        both late night and early morning reincarnating
It was a candidate planet
Different physics   you could fly   had the talent

A lesson more than scales and chords
        and coming close to playground matters

The dream interprets *itself*
Auspices
With patronage
        assurance and suggestion
                a bigger backyard
You'll go to the Cannon Beach Library
Find the book *Between Pacific Tides*

We used to love to play
We'll play in the sea   married or otherwise

Then the teacher gave the *student* an apple
        a russet

nobody happier
There were also sardines

The first dream of Cannon Beach was like a chiaroscuro
Done while the unseen clams
        including *Solen sicarius*
                dig down deeply
                and pray to the moon
                        that it stay in its orbit
                        entirely attracted to the earth
Just like the seastacks

The nocturnal bluff part of a protected outer shore
And I was protected   in turn   by my teacher
        then and always:
"You want a pink Cadillac you'll need to knuckle down"

There were other admonitions   ruthful
We were a colony of two generations
        so west of the Rockies
                no postcard could tell it

The dream would have its anniversary
        again and again
A *lottery* of dreamtime
Each installment curving into vista
                the ephemeral bluff and lookout
                whatever else is going on

Something to make us smart as scallops
Clever, even   able to Google next century
        so that danger's an innocence of Satan's hidden away

There's a road to get to it
You're always allowed
        no lethal force is ever required

Later   wading   first guess
A jellyfish in the nearshore tide!
        what to *do*?!   so very awkward!
A book half a century later
        will say it could have been *sessile Haliclystus*

You had to see through the suds of broken waves

to see them   a visual thing

They do what they do for their god
And I   a recusant   stumble in the brine
Which way to go?
        a case of the nerves

"Oh, don't worry about them…"
        somebody sure of themselves
Saying we are not sea life   only visitants
Though the salt water left in the blood belies

Never liked the looks of them
Non-solid   non-moral   non-elect creatures
        was this thing dead or alive?

The water was like green cellophane
                wanting to wrap you
                as if something had suddenly come to power
An arch enemy fluid
        whose minion jellies serve to distract

Sang a song just then
        with a note-of-note's recurring pitch
Song of going away
And being borne back to a hallowed hallway
        in the year of *endless* high school hallways

You made it to the moon
And *back* to moon jellies
        knees knocking knee-deep in the Humboldt tide
Belonging to no one
                but danger's plans for you

Close to the oh-so-sharp barnacles
I spoke and even sung
        to the shellfish
        news of marine life
                glued to newspaper rocks conceived by Bruegel
And pictured Zone 3 of all 5 seashore levels

The anemones are large
And lawyered up with prospective attorneys
        family trials   revelations

Be careful!   the razor clams   your hands!
Be *studious*-careful
        though the basalt patiently waits for inspection
        and loves the sound of conversation
                has heard the grieving of relatives
                reliving family history

The Haystack's made Saint Mark's for the moment
A force of nature barely contained
The memory of stone
        crossing over it such
                each human recollection
                        is a next door neighbor of today

Still a secret

Yet present as the fishing boat
        backing into concealment
Quiet enough for the second person to speak
                a tense well-suited

Green eyes
Green sea-sad
        born and raised
                what's going to happen?

Oh, clamber like a cocky robot on the colonized boulders!
        small business done
Man the jellyfish observation platform
Pretend to have nearly died

Mortality   handheld like a falcon   is cradled
In all the salt sea
        what's a little more blood
                and cuts the black razor makes?
But I *do* feel safe for now

Wish the terrier hadn't come
Out of loyalty he's splashed out here to too much danger
In fact there's an *entourage* of animals
        beachcombing also
                their heroic hearts
                in support of the careless humans

Tide turning?
How much time?
Who's going to care?

It's an artful shore
        the next poem milling about
        waiting for an ancient scholar to write it down
Down *deep*   and then release the words
As life on earth and Altair IV

No one's stranded
Well, not yet
        but your little island's about to drown
                in the next ninth wave

Autonomous   self-rescue
From the transparency afloat

Who we are is saved for later fiction
The fact of jellyfish in the sea had made me afraid
        but when it's over?
                anemones green!
                and anemones blue!

Haystack's a holy place undone
A ravaged chapel
        populated with brilliant strangers
        who had so much to say
                they had to be a color
For shame!   for shame!

The underwater flowers go to college
To divinity school
The moment you meet them
        they seem to say things   *unisono*
        whimpering in the dormitory pool
                and playing watery guitars
They're cramming

A final before the spring break of exposure

There isn't time for a love song
        maybe a *like* song, though

key of Cannon Beach
They sing for their breakfast
                              lunch
                              and dinner
Being so voracious *anything* will do!

Squish!   squirt!
It's an introductory offer

Is it possible to *be* these things somehow?
Don't do your homework you'll be turned into one!

My mother   so early on the travel day:
"It's going to be good!"
        she said it in the kitchen
        4 a.m.
                bacon to go and get me going
She was happy at least *one* of us would see the beach

Then the azure dawn in the window's sky!
Like the blue of anemones to come
        sea-blue
                early start
She delivered her son to the teacher
                when they might travel south away

Before the beach was known
                and the *Anthopleura elegantissima*
In the prelude morning no fugue imagined
Nor Scriabin's ecstatic rainbows

Arriving   the beach was every instrument
The City of Sound you thought you saw
        in a mysterious movie once
                when
                because of the movie camera
                        the orchestra seemed a town
All its hundreds and hundreds of citizens playing

And a mayor conductor

That was the music city I always wanted to live in
Hearing white noise symphonies
        performed by light-fingered personnel

prepared to steal only what's wondrous!

Contemplate the pool again
        in which the sea anemones open as if for a payday
A parliament too   apart from the people
Their ensembles
                quartets tingling
                nettle effects
                hands-on!

What just happened?!
Double take   it's alive!
They're *all* alive and evading   vignetting

They're the creatures in the messy mirror
On the shockproof shore
                                pitiless
                                inclement
Their tentacles are sensitive
        but inured to biological suffering

An hour ago they'd been unknown
But then   in a washbasin bowl of politesse
        soaking I saw them
        staring
                part of an otiose enterprise of amateur collectors

A trillion beings like themselves to go one-stop shopping
And no matter *what* you want to do
        the anemones delay the doing
        as they gaze   colorized

Have I said how utterly hypnotic it was
Breathing in the presence
                soft toys
                don't touch
                        though you have the opportunity?

I wish Bela Bartok were here
With a whole quartet to serenade these things
I'm just entering puberty
        and too distracted to properly serenade the anemones

No aria for the *actiniaria*

Though the lure of the Latin is strong
    an ancient language
    that lends freshness to *tete-à-tetes*

The teacher of more than music attends
It is more than mere attachment
             more halfway to heaven
No fathers or nuns follow after

Oh, the saintly starfish wearing orange lipstick!
Soon as I saw them it was like a salty outreach
Beings belonging to rocks from another world
    the sunshine the same as Altair IV's
    Haystack's assemblage
      part of a scrim of the forbidden fourth planet out

And one of my friends
    with astronomical wits
      had said
      after the movie appeared:

"There could never be an earth-like planet about that star!
Wrong color   too hot   too many ultraviolet rays!"

But here's the planet
Painted again
    and harboring the Id
"Id, id, id, id, id!"
    the obsolete term that Morbius explained

But these are the outtakes
The world before the water dried
      body/mind   mind/body
      before those terms had lost their way

Wouldn't mind a firefight with the Krell
Provided I have more than a mere three billion electron volts
What a contest would our battle be!
    with no desire to harm the puzzle we've put together

It takes a teacher to say, "Cease fire!"
    and so we will
    there was a breather
 Earth had never seemed more of a planet

than when it was a forbidden beach
with invisible monsters

There was a cove
A grotto of boulders gray
        and ledges
        and rockfalls
Perfect place for stranded pebbles
Or a visit from Space
            when you're lost and lonesome

Place where the waves are hidden away
In a sandstone theater's recess
Pounds and tons   undermining minerals
        everybody waiting on erosion
            strange echoes and acoustics
Sound erased like the seastacks

Some things don't go together
I'm staying here to find out why
        with a simple camera held unsteadily

"Snap"   "take"   "capture"
"Click" looking out
        "click"   the second Needle included
Devils and angels of the air: "click"
The basaltic wall   wide-angle
            G Minor promising more

This isn't home
Not yet   I'm too nervous

"Snap"   hand-held and blurring
It would soon be a seascape
        greatly enlarged once it was developed
        and expressed on butcher paper
            with #1 lead

A camera's glance of diagonal lines
An unsteady shot carefully copied
        the blowup shaded
            according to the well-worn glossy
            grid lines drawn to clarinet squeaks

Black-and-white as the instrument
Shiny gray as the bowling pencil conceives it
A painstaking spectacle
        and mysterious
                to your sisters
                        and mother
                                and father

They wonder what dilemma this is
        that must be so grandly rendered
        and done no other way
And the giant picture so lovingly shaded
                every sound
                and all the days of its being drawn
                        are included in the canvas

Thirteen-year-old eyesight took over
The wrong end of the telescope
Mega-sketch
        of a new best friend called Cannon Beach
        its cove in the Haystack fully realized

It was delicate
And I stroked the white parchment
        so much made of a blurry solitude
                when the jiggled camera blinked
                while I stood uncertainly

Amidst tumbled stone stairs and chairs a jerky "click"
Too late in the day to be careful
        and step everywhere you *wanted* to step

So the sea appeared and disappeared in the aperture
Until the one careless composition came
        its teenage vocabulary enough for obsession
        for talk about birds and kelp

And the Big Picture   as it came to be called
        from the small one made
        would be left unfinished
                the labor left alone
                as too perfectionist an art
It would be gone
Or about to be lost

the vast panorama from a small black-and-white

Stored for awhile in the little hobby shop prior to college

What do I mean?
Something important unfinished
And you'd have it back somehow
        opening *Between Pacific Tides*
        exactly there
                with all its color plates

But nothing the Brownie could see that day that special way
Shaky sepia conjured as part of the past
The ocean's unnerving prehistory told as wild dreams
        dreams *within* dreams
        playing hard-to-get in the waking dawn
                yet dedicated to sunrise
                and footsteps to the sea
                        come from the crossroads

The next dream was another night
And a storm was in it
A cauldron centered on that same Haystack
        so wild at first I misunderstood

"What do you want?"   asked aloud
The storm spray in the cove illumined with klieg lights
        white salt lace stretched
        to be a Cinerama's windy wide-angle
No plot to its shipwrecked moment

Lay in the dream dark seeing things you never saw
Hearing things you didn't say
                or thought to say later

The bright storm was *elasticized* light
        that banished apathy
        with the first line spoken by the romantic lead
No story told at the movies
In a movie made in '49 on a modest budget

The small screen pulled apart
        when Bogart turns to Bacall
                and asks her something he already knows

Singing somewhere his heart is

Camera coming close
     Action in the North Atlantic
     all the hurricane flics
          swirling   dangerous!

This evening it could happen again
White water in the gray-black grotto
"Lights!"   "Camera!"
     in the cauldron bowl of Doctor Death
         and sorrow
         and freight train winds!

When you may forget to wake up
     from the roar
     and rounding of pebbles
Their punishment a death rattle in the slanted air

So I sang that song again
Colored the foam
Made lucid the shadowed scrawl
     pirouetting
     the outer coast surrendered to scintillating light
Stage-lit   the white light conceptual

In the listing of thoughts   foremost was chaos
I kept singing awake
     a proposition put to the soul
         swimming in the mind to inaccessible reefs
         barely three-dimensional

At the Ecola Inn's restaurant's window
     thinking in Italian
     the language to be attempted as part of the future
Keeping quiet the while

The smaller pinnacles attending Haystack
Dangerous as the heroin you've heard tell of
"On the rocks"
     as much as anyone may be in venturing there

Beyond first grade's first day
When I couldn't get enough of its revolutionary lacquer

its janitorial polish

What landfall
        into landfall
        and shoal
        and sharpened slivers!
God has made a wrecking place
     of hammered stone and cemetery surf

Sugar shock of a chocolate shake
     while the clam diggers dig
         with imperfect knowledge
            of the wet sand's citizens' exact whereabouts
Sweet shore!
The milkshake *cold* and giving headaches

And all the sharpened disgrace
Solid black remnants not the least bit whole
     the basalt twisted almost cowlick-macabre!

Like an idea destroyed
Replaced by dark conjecture
     deeply separate
        and at such a young age
        all of Nature in the crag's solid cage
An igneous density

Gallows stone
Philosopher's stone
     designed for youthful minds
     the seascape conscious
The ocean and the boy
       watching each other
       for evidence of a Christian reality

In all of this adrenalin there ought to be a cat!
In the store part of Ecola Inn
A cat to purr and go with all the comforts
     and telling the tide tables
       and time of day to study the sea
       as if it were a film

And what was about to be seen was so beautiful
     you'd make it a *job*   without pay

First job in the world of employment

Sip the shake
And observe the way the breakers break
        on a blank silhouette
Sing the refrain again
                in the key of unauthorized
                        unutterable longings

Reenter the third dream
The one that was *ascent* of the formidable
        the story to include acrophobia
            all of its freezing
            in the midst of those birds' nests!

You   in the sanctuary of demon birds
They say they're dinosaurs
        derived from the Jurassic
                thunder lizards
                velociraptors   *et alia*

Keep going to the apex   attacked en route
Go up to screams
        the birds and your own!
Like a song so new it's the very first version

Cry out for silence   no rescue required
I'm happy to stay aloft
                comfortable
                no downclimbing to come

"Hey, everybody!   look up here!
I don't need to come down!
Don't worry!   I'm fine!   just fine!
    send the helicopter *back*"

Thought-words and all their meanings
Meaning to fly away
        like these gray-and-white guys
Because I've done that in dreams
                                just like this one

Welcome acrophobia!
In well-worn tennies

and they're not the right shoes
Be careful of the bird nests!
                                        and don't look down!
It's entirely too windy
                    I'll blow away

Buddy Holly's singing "That'll Be The Day"
Their antique Crickets' guitars
        sound from far away as a broken heart
        forget-me-not notes
                    flowers of the mind and memory

Insights ascending the forbidden rock
Lucid-delayed till wake up
        you return to Miocene years
                disciplined by improbable nuns
                at the summit of their powers of persuasion
Habits in a habitat

Went way beyond the sign:
"Do Not Go Beyond This Point!"
        for a past life said to do just that
It was the future you'd find
                        thirteen years into the present
                        doing dizzy acrobats

It was an Egyptian height above the Giza Plateau
Grateful for the pyramid you climbed
        the better to appreciate flat sand later
        the mud flat plain with its mirror finish
            going two-dimensional, even
                notwithstanding the presence of solid geometry

Take the wide wet highway to Hug Point's palace
Learn its source of salty revenue
        being young enough to gallop there
        gallop like the horses   and go missing

Your teacher worried like a superior court judge

Hug Point   the place to be a part of
Be in favor of a reconnaissance
Pick up the signal from a Model T
        rounding the uneven bend

oh, there is more than one
and they are caravanning

"I don't care what color as long as it's black!"
Henry Ford   American motor man
        goes to sleep at the wheel of karma
        searching for like-minded in Germany
            with industrial yearning

At Hug Point they carved a road in the rock
For his motorcar
        and it's still a path for me and you
            at the southern extreme
            of all the cannon's field of fire

We're so all right   right where we need to be
With ample opportunity to go missing
        they went missing too
            who were paid five dollars a day
            assembling the country

Hallelujah!   for the sake of shouting in the wind!
Four hours in the House of Outdoors!
        the wayfaring stranger's desire
            he doesn't care to come back till supper

How long would a piano stay in tune out here?
Where's the Bumble?
        the Bee?
            the Tuna today?
We're looking *everywhere*
                    in all the ups and downs around

And I had a feeling
It would *not* be the last time a search was made
Feeling like a shaking all over
        as though the whole universe knew a new set of rules
        and Hug Point's the point

No regrets the buggies are bygone
A transport slyly overlying later on
Their ghosts go by   by the way
        put my thumb out "thumbing for a hitch"
            like in the song from *Oz*

Wishing to travel to innovative destinations
South   north
        not to mention the *inland* places
The journeys to start with a song
            the same sung since all this arrival

Look into it!
The lyrics to come
        the heart your home the length of the day

Barnacles   limpets   and tires   together
Ledge as roadway for a roadshow
An auto show of see-through chassis

Death doesn't wait and works up an appetite
Skinny as I am
        and *hungry*-skinny
            I start to look for scraps
            like the cormorants and terns

Taking names at the edge of Elk Creek

Crossing over the creek
Once "Elk"
        now-and-later the Indian word for a whale
        "Ecola"
The same that Sacagawea came to see
            in the company of Lewis and Clark

Can be "Elk Creek" for now   for history
Elk Creek in time for dinner, then
        the white birds all in a row
        a lineup now no more
            their imploring beauty
                            that has a body

A favorite poetic passage
Award-winning birds
        released on the day of your marriage
And the creek called "Elk"
            is what God learned in Creation's forest

A teacher's gift of one August

that touches evolution
        and piano technique
        just all the ceremonies of practice
Words to say the music
        flowing under the little white bridge

Was an elk seen one day   someone fishing
        and *that* comprised the naming?
Ever after it had to be "Elk Creek?"
Was its watershed populated with more elk than most?

Ice cream and cake
        to go with this speculation
Then be guided up the stream with ice-cold feet
On porous platforms amidst the pebbles

Hear the chorus that accompanies all of your baby talk
        born again though once was enough

There are thousands of feathers
And little creek cliffs
            in dream time
                a tribe of one
                and chamber chorus of uncountable loves

Every upstream meadow
        is here transported to the salt
        a movie called *hydrology* running
Let's see how many birds the cake crumbs summon
            to Elk Creek's banks
                with its dried kelp
                and sand fleas

Look it up in the little library
Something short enough
        to be read entirely to the laughter of fools
Look up Lewis   look up Clark   and the whale
        "Ecola" called

Sacajawea longed to see it
And exactly *how* was it said?
        what syllable was stressed?

Be in the aisles

Changing names before it closes
        tidy as any small cottage
                cozy as improvised shelter
The trees read while the rain falls down the sky

And you find thirteen years
        are enough to know a disciplined hour
Same as the music hour the teacher taught
And now the music day and night in Oregon

It's inside the outside entering the library
Small truths coaxed into print
        so that   for a time
                you hold the answers to all the teacher's questions

Hey!   where is he, anyway?
                        what's he doing?

Wish there was a way to get the books' contents
        just by touching their titles
        being Vulcan-tactile enough
Ideas taking the place of long time ago
The way this library's a little Alexandria
                anywhere the myths are safekept

Got a feeling the librarian likes me
We're dreaming together a temporary Egypt
        the many gifts of the pharaoh
        alleged by the Dewey Decimal System
                the reading cursory

It was a *Bell, Book and Candle* place
Like a store with books
Half an hour to closing
        coming there was indirection
                proving I got it wrong somehow
                in spite of a reading room

It was 1957   in the center of the century almost

Antenna fingers
        finding out for half an hour
        in the slanting sunshine
                over the carpet come

to bewilder the mind with bloodshot

Pretend the books are notebooks spiraled
The tilt of light
        saddening the scholar's day of blank pages
                that flutter
                while one lusts after local history read as fiction

It's still prior to closing
        the negative of opening
                but begone
                it's time to return
To the Bug's Ear Motel?
No, the Blue Gull Inn!   think that's the one

Can a gull be blue?
One morning there
        is enough awakening
                to get through college
                and dissemble as respectable
An attorney, perhaps

This coast is the best show business ever seen
        the blue gull in command
And are you sure it's not another life?

Leave a message at the Inn
Say you'll help the teacher shop
                for he loves souvenirs
Does *he* think there's a blue gull somewhere?

Have decided it's Mothers Day
        even though the calendar says no
Wonderful was the breakfast she made
        for this going away to see the cannon

Since it's an extra day in her honor
        we'll souvenir *her* as well with a greeting
"Thank you!"
I'm only a teen   but "Thank you, mom!"

There's no piano in town
Wherever we go
        down lanes with open cottage doors

No Timothy Leary, either
Oh, no   not yet!
        it's still "That'll Be the Day"

And why does Buddy Holly follow me around?
It's like The Crickets have taken rooms at the Blue Gull Inn

All I know is
        the tune accompanies every walk
            "...when you say goodbye"
Splatting the brown wet level mud
In time to "the day that'll be"
                    the refrain like an engram

The blue gull's a chaperone bird
I've decided I'm retired too
        like the many seniors hereabouts
And the Inn's good karma is caught

Pretend to be a moron
Maybe an alternate Churchill
        young and misguided
            and challenged by no ambition

Whatever happens
        stay on the good side of your piano teacher
After all, he paid for this Inn
        placed bets on the blue gull
        as if it were a coastal casino of one game only
Entertained his students!
Rolled the dice of holiday

But I'm onto him
The house always wins
        house of room numbers
                            cash in
                            check out

And Steve   funny bone berzerk   loving it!
Like I did in study hall
        and all those assemblies
            when you're supposed to be quiet
The library the same: "Shhhh!"

Cloud secrets   kid freak-outs
You never knew what might set it off
                an eyebrow
                a look
                a noise
Giggles from nowhere
And the harder you try *not* to...

The teacher was only too familiar with this
At *concerts* he'd paid for
Right in the middle of the master's pianissimo
        the insuppressible giggle
        gone a little crazy and helpless!

And the laughter would spread to the other students
Mozart squeals
The music abandoned
        for cadenzas in the balcony
                and a virgin's appeal to the gods of comedy

"Make it *stop*, someone!
Make it stop, oh please!
He brought us to the concert
        we *have* to be quiet somehow"
                "Shhh!"
                "Don't!"
                "Don't start   don't do that again!"

All whispers   desperate   hysterical
This would happen over and over!

Then there was the aftermath after dark
        the opposite of giggling
        Cannon Beach   serious   alone
                                except for the sea

And can you tell it's getting closer?
Coming in?
Take away the fear
        thirteen years are enough for that

In the Blue Gull Inn   so beautifully appointed
        I should be fast asleep in the night
                but there's another "Shhh!" going on

So be quiet for other reasons

There might be a transhuman
          a Krell out there
          maybe he's a giant
Out there in the surf
                    the sound a perfection of morphemes
                    heavenly white in the night

Pretend it's Australia
Some other shore
I can only tell you it felt so peaceful
          suspended
                    a pedagogy so beyond Beyond
                    the piano's left behind

This music   this sound of the breakers
And being beautifully not sure of anything at all
          except the teacher asleep
                    a mysterious safety
                    in the guardian night
                              the sheets skin-tight
                              and fresh as a miracle

Learn that the word "panegyric"
          describes what I wanted to say securely
Listen carefully
High tide   noise within noise
                    a ninth wave now and then
Beautiful radio   beautiful hiss!

Before credit cards and the internet
          there was the static ocean all night long
And it made the room a cradle   candlelit

I thought of phosphorescent light
The way the breakers brighten
          unmistakingly
          but dimly
                    is it plankton?

There's science in the surf out there
Science and emptiness
          a shockingly cold blanket

        trying to cover us discarded creatures

You know, it's almost like dim sparks
Beyond thinking hidden thoughts
A make-believe glow
      of liquid fairies *inside* the sea!
         and it's been so long
         I could barely believe they'd resumed

The single loudest sound made a hush
And not only is there a sorcery of *water*
      there's singing in the sand
      what a whisper's susurrus says

"What are you running from?"

And you can *just* hear its conspiracy
Keeping on into:
    "Listen!   *Ecoute*!"
Do you hear it?
Wait for the wind
         like memory
         one more truth

Yes, listen!
The perfect pitch of a ghost going by
      what physics longs to explain
        and it's making me sleepy
        sleepier
          the sleepiest audience

Listen!   the sand is making music!
I would drink and dance to it in the sixties
     in homes and bars
     with every one that Carol knew
She was the girl that came later
        with wine
         and a later piano

The isolated instrument leaning
      at the edge of a very loud party
        when playing it was noiseless
        unheard   unlearned   unpedaled music
Its notes a puzzle of hammers and strings

What to play in the midst of merry relatives

Other times ducking into a lounge
        to be a big spender
While a romance stalled between Washington and California
And I was unlearning Czerny and Hanon

Learning instead the quarter rest
                the half
                and the whole
A dream of this
Prescience and foreboding
                in the bars of a beach town
                years after all the footprints were made

Bars as black as Haystack's stone
Their dark interiors
        plush
        lush
Let's go in!   let's go back
                the Civil War less than a century fought

Remember Lincoln in the drunken dark
The lighthouse president
Drink to that   to anything you say
        we're kids getting older one bar at a time

Say the two words "Cannon Beach"
        before they're lost to liquor
Propose to me a toast   your heart is my own
And we will never leave this latitude and longitude!

Wait for the day it snows again   sea level
Wait for the tsunami from Cascadia's subduction trench

So you take her down deep
        as if into a well
Diving together every time we listen to certain voices

Contrast   the first principle of art applied
Beach boy to barfly   the lounge as experiment
        when you circulate like water in the cave
                sloshing the starfish
                Pisaster ochraceus

A certain degree of sophistication

What are you *doing*, future student?
Your fiancee needs no alcohol
        its molecules alien as Altair's hopes and dreams

There are many waterfalling destinies
Adapt the hands
        find the only grip possible
                on enemy rock controlled by the moon
Key to any problem   drinking or otherwise

"You need to leave!"

Say it just the way the bartender tells it
To *yourself* say it
        issue the challenge
                do the right thing in the years to come
                barefoot   muddy

An ideology extended
Your misbehavior labeled correctly
It's all about the preservation of dreams
                the hazards of not doing so!

For sobriety remembers
Remembers into a.m.
        the night to process the cannon
                its realm of ammunition
Remembers the dream of the outsized seastacks

Reading a volume the size of a coffee table's
A picture book of Space Shuttles to come

Saying something about the basalt towers
"It was in 1948 the rock fell apart…"
        one less Needle
        a before and an after

It showed
In colors close to the blues of what was seen
        all that was left
                and left to fall some future day

I was aware of a certain magnification
Haystack Rock and all of the rest
     a supersized ensemble
        and there were tunnels everywhere

Nothing solid   see-through forts
And I entered the nearest recent excavation
Fresh surfaces exposed   uncolonized
     like whatever happened today
        being rushed into print
        or a hard-bound brochure

Imagining Israel about to be born
And it's that fifties show, "You Are There"
Thank the dream maker mind
     some morning
     under a million mile wide sun

Approach Chapman Bluff
     see if he's home
        bring a message from the teacher who couldn't come
Chapman the northern boundary of Cannon

Make it an essay   the reconnaissance
All the climbing and falling down
Let it be something you think of all the time
     a definition of freedom
     first teen year and spacetime sea

And Christmas green
        going on
        and going over the bluff
Seeing Tillamook
The lighthouse
     the headland
        closer than ever
        from the alley of pebbles close by the cliffs

Take time to appreciate the work of the sun
     warming stone benches
     and all the angles of that igneous playpen
No hurry   no mistakes   keep the camera dry
     until you are done with danger

The principles of correct fingering applied to clambering
Even here at Chapman
        the right touch
                delicate even

The black geometry warm and jagged
These are the rough platforms fishermen use
        and a father and son are arranged
        smartly and safely elevated
Teaching in progress

The bait   the cast
It's a detour to see them
                and say my name
                my own teacher's too

A pleasant conversation
There on the sunny side of the tricky blocky terrain
        in whose watery creases creatures skitter

We were various bones in motion
And getting hungry
        in this corner of Crypto Mundo to come

Someone's induced the shore to be shades of gray
"Click!" for your mother
For Mister Short   the piano teacher has a name
"Click!"   "Click!"
        another roll
        deep in the branches above the rocks

I'm Buddy Holly shooting for his album
In enormous topographies
        losing the light
                finding other paths past other houses
From Chapman's heights back down to the beach
More inland than out

Satisfied the coast goes north
        I'm both Lewis and Clark in one scrawny body
                and worried about Sacagawea
Able to say there's more of the same beyond Beyond

For Crescent Beach continues

Curvature on curvature after that
    you can barely believe such beauty!
Would you mind if I show you tomorrow?

Tonight we'll see the cave again
With flashlights searching for monsters
    in the little schoolhouse of clams and limpets
      the movie star anemones
        the unfailing fish
        toiling at their schoolwork

Hear come the kids again after dark
To hear that stone's instruction
    hear the school bell for recess
Sightless   except for the camera's white-electric light

Like the appearance of momentary angels
All smiles in a color-blind tunnel

"What did you see in there?
What did you see?"
    in the sand-choked grotto
      saved the best for last
      walking in boots on out to sea
        through unfamiliar underground breakers

Beyond a dark window tell the truth
Half-man half-boy half-beast
    waiting there
    a mysterious combination
      in a summer cave composed
      with barely perceived ultraviolet walls
Whispering demons *in situ*

It is the most temporary shelter and dragon's lair
Two years we waited
    to be in the lesser waves of a minus 2.1
    rarest low!

That all this cave and more besides
    could be revealed
      like a long-lost nightmare
A minus-minus   like pre-tsunami's retreat
Mossy and disfigured pisasters

It is ritual slime
        and death is squishy underfoot!

Let us click the crime scene and bouldered atrocities
"Click!"   the intermittent lantern
                                wearing ancient sandals

In the morning more horses and pedal carts
A Chinese alley's worth
        and horses' reflections approaching
        somehow shining

I fell in love with them again and again
Cried in broad daylight
        the horses' shadows shining
                on their flat wet pasture
                    no horseshoes required!

"If I ride you will you make me a captive and gallop away?"

We'll be mirrored inhabitants and cross the glass together
Caravanning southwards
        on the silk road past Jockey Cap
        and the Lion   crouching
                knights of the castle of Castle Rock
                whose moat is all of the Pacific!

Barefoot   horse and rider
Make it distant Colorado again
        asleep in the saddle
                the Coast Range the Front Range
                with its sunken mesas

Horse be "Babe," the backyard stallion
Let loose finally
        from the outskirts of the windy Renton Highlands
Recite "That horse whose rider fears to jump will fall"
        the line from a poem
        in a long-lost poetry book

I'd say, "Horsie, horsie!"
Even after getting thrown
        horsie with the biggest eyes you ever saw
                you were "Amazing Grace"

beyond a gospel choir's say-so

Break free of break-in!
Be an Ice Age horse
        horse before Haystack built an Oregon Island

Or summon the Dawn horsie in the ambient blue
"Eohippus" called
        with blue above and blue below
        blue between the silver and white

The clouds are elongate
Becoming summery
        you wander with access
            access   what I'm talking about!
Almost dying, characteristically
In a Middle School of steep and crumbly places

I've not enough money to stay here
At the cafe on the corner
        the fantasies pour a protest
        long, long ago utensils in the sun
The counter *warm* for an hours-long breakfast

It is a plain undecorated diner
I'll start using my own money someday
        buy the teacher a pancake in the very first teenage year
He said he buys a new car every three years

It is two days so far without Chopin
Will the composer be mad
        "Barnacles, Frederic!
        they are so sharp!   piano hands!"

More walking   faster and faster
And singing again
        "That'll Be The Day"   perfect
            a happiness expanding outwards
Those days that were two weeks long!

It seemed as though the sea
        and everything in it
            was sharply drawn
Binocular vision and being alone

done exactly right

There's a motif to Cannon Beach
And Mister Short   the ex-marine
        was a strangely foreign father
        but friendly every occasion we met

My trust in him had allowed this reconnaissance
A pre-bibulous thing
        standing on the platforms left
                when the wet sea sinks and recedes
Wondering why I can only further dream in *this* dream

Heel-to-toe motion erosion
The only place for fathers' Day
Let's hop into a pedal cart
        get some speed up
                for a dash to Silver Point and back

Be in and out of the Pacific puddle
Go that far and revolutionize the world!
        right along with Khrushchev
There's a Sputnik somewhere
                "Beep-beep-beep…"

Pretend it's the Black Sea before you
        and the first satellite's falling on the city of Sebastopol

"We have to get outta' here!
Faster, faster!"
        ride these things anywhere
The surf comes back and all the sea life there is

And we are between those Pacific tides
Between the town of Renton
        and the rock they call the Jockey Cap
What do they mean?
Do *you* see a hat?   how is it a hat?

"Let's climb the nearby tower!
It's so doable
        there's a path to the top   c'mon!
Look, it's easy   like prosperity
And we're going to be rich if we get to the top!

"The Jocky Cap's too dangerous
        but this climb's just right
                anybody could do it safely
Let's charge a toll
This could be Haystack   we'll say it *is*

"Look!   how green the green is!
Grab on
        that's it
                all the way!
View the Cap from above
This Jockey next door to be a favorite!"

I wonder about that jockey
Some kid like me?
        or Spanish Riding School?
                super-professional perhaps
                no answers
What jockey?
What cap removed as a courtesy?

The words we know are missing
The exact discourse with my friend
He's not here to teach the history of our conversation
        what we students talked about in August

Though I'm sure it was intentional dialogue
Intentional as all the dreams that came
The one about the *barn*
        the monolith as part of a farmyard of stones

It was another walkabout
The Haystack uncovered once more
        by an abnormally low tide
And while we stumbled in the mud
        and slipped on the gleaming kelp
                we could see into interiors
                and knew the Haystack was hollow that held the hay

Just a glance was all
We were cheating the tide and had to keep moving
        as far out to sea
                without the water

we'd ever been
and gotten back to tell it

The fishermen were so beyond their fishing ground waves
their "See ya later!" was a lie
They'll be a postcard to buy in Ecola Inn
When you shop
when you go
and later go to bed

The Lion is yellow like the veldt
Turned to African sandstone
and crouched to pounce upon the land
All the times he tries I'll be there
grabbing his blocky mane
wondering if he's a *dry* food or a *wet* food cat

And if being stone makes "nine lives" a moot question

I'd been searching for a pet like this
The southern boundary rock
for what we'll call the cannon's purview and field of fire
What is planned behind closed doors

Later I dreamed the ocean dry
With parallel lines westward to a vanishing
It was a set from *Tales of Hoffmann*
with ballet to the famous "Barcarolle"

They dance   then slowly walk to the seafloor's horizon
Where a sunset's opacity is a distant orange
will we ever see the end?
Their *pas-de-deux* relaxed
she's escorted beyond the peculiar sculptures

Odd towers that teeter
under the influence of the art of the fifties
with diaphanous banners

The house that Morbius built
as a stage for alien melodrama
The dancers desert the paradox
And are ballet step-by-step
to all that orange infinity's convergence

Surely Offenbach awaits
And E.T.A. Hoffmann looks on from off-world wings
        enjoying the cinematic attention

Oh, help us understand
        how such artistry of lines suffice for all of the Pacific!
Help us to know how such a dream may recur
        and Cannon Beach become a home
                for the directors Powell and Pressburger
                        persuaded to stay
                        and stay local

Their *own* dreams added to our own

Turn towards Tillamook
The rock island reworked to accommodate a house
        a lens
        a light
                that turns
                dizzy as science itself
                        frenetic   last minute

Last August for a live-in keeper keeping on

"Olly olly oxen free!"
Like a summons to supper
        last supper
        last summons
He has to come in after all that sun and rain

On the rock called Tillamook Light
        it will be "*Adieux*!"
                to the cleft that so indented the little island
"*Adieux*!" to the breeches buoy for coming and going
"*Adieux*!" to such magnificent solitude
        they'd make of it a columbarium later

"Do Not Disturb" the ashes brought
The urns a business
        like ironic moths attending the replacement beam
        converging on an artificial Pharos
                still fiery!

I am motivated to go to it
On one of those days
    when the ocean's a lake with barely a swell
Just land the inner tube there
And fully trespass   no matter the outcome

Some industry of childhood
Make it night
    and I'll be the kid that's calm
    in calm conditions
        come to enact the rituals of all the lightkeepers
A flashlight for a light

What a pleasure that would be!
To man the lighthouse again
    privately   surreptitiously
      light for the ashen moths
      an innovation
        a nocturnal cartoon

How the old days may be old when they were brand new
Like the zigzag of the highway entering town
    first, the little white bridge
      then your left
      your right

Like future army commands
    converted to directions to Les Shirley
      the park
      and rockaby moments past the post office
Shingled gray
Unassuming
    so as not to upstage the ocean

And mostly quiet out of respect for the nearby breakers

Think there was lumber for sale
And lovely stories
    almost whispered
    between the clotheslines
      strung among enchanted chimneys

Think there was room at the Bug's Ear
What a beautiful day

that day we twisted and turned
        the last quarter mile to enter the village
        and yield to its Kryptonite

Weak in a good way
As if it were your first major scale besides C
Just getting into it
                the flats
                the sharps
                the naturals

Who was he, anyway?
Why did I love him so?
Perhaps his conspicuous kindness and endless patience
        his attention to detail
        how he made his students stop
                if they were in too big a hurry

How he knew the cannon would change our lives
And be a balm for helpless youth
        stranded between "horse" and "horsie"
His voice was an ironing in this world of wrinkles
                hot silver in his luminous instruction

He'd be at the the side of the road
Renton to all points south
Be there on the ferry
        Megler to the piers of Astoria
Be there standing in
        for a student's fall-apart appearance onstage

So that no one's betrayed
So that you think of best friends more than anything else

"What did you do when you were a marine?"
        (but of course a marine is *always* a marine!)
"Went to Nicaragua"
"How long ago?   how long?"
"1926"
He said that if he'd ever concertized
        he'd have played his concerts with a crew cut

His lessons
        were like the learning received

from a black-and-white view of Ecola State Park
Notes on the page of music
        the notes of Albeniz's pages of "Iberia"
        the ink good shades of goodbye-and-bye

Is there any Mozart left to practice?
All written already?
The artistry and the era
        fragile as shells put to the ear
                as conch telephones

As if to place an order for the creature lately vanished
The composer   the shellfish
        a sand dollar down
                temporary housing
                delicately furnished

Believe in shells of the *past*
Even Rome had a hinge   was two-part
The western empire and all of the eastern
        starting with Constantinople
                shell of the Mediterranean

Up and down the shore
        who knew antiquity would know such a thin replication
Would be a bivalve   a bifurcation?

And the year I saw the place?
A Crate Paper day of exquisite sheaves

I need to name the stones
        before naming's no longer an urgency

Perhaps the last thing to do   if there *is* a last
        will be to dream of Cannon Beach while I'm there
        for it was the epicenter of something
                you know not what absolutely

But perhaps that synthesis
The mind asleep in the very cradle it imagines
The cave become a columbarium's formal internment

Formed a government in going
Carpe deum!

a sea kayak some placid day of sky-high pressure
        its ridge and rudimentary weather

Touring the backside of Haystack Rock
The steepest side of all
        floating into the sea cave
        what you always wanted to do
A little at a time   low tide again
        the *only* tide for that

With "Neptune, the Mystic" sounding
Just barely
        those sopranos so remote
            they might be the wives
            yes, the wives of all those
                                    "presidents"
            we've seen as street names in town

Washington   Adams   Jefferson
The *first* presidents branching off of Hemlock Road

Enter the cave from the sea
        to all those sounds of careful paddling
Like a Soviet Luna   discovering
Looping around to see the few farside maria of the moon
            Tsiolkovsky
            The Sea of Moscow

The spaceship had shown us in 1959!
First view!   first fly-past!
It was televised
        new highlands
            the backside seen

The future would come to Cannon Beach
And sleeping in the same bed   early
        the color tan is a secret wall

The farside face that faces a fifties sea
With fishing boats
        bobbing uncertainly
I'm hiding   it's a hideout
Place that was always dry in the dream
Place where you'd walk all around

and once or twice clamber on the rock itself

And Haystack Rock rose at an oasis
A hill with pines   spruce
                              and queenslace
An isle
      the *Isle of the Dead* heard
      dead   or at least asleep

And while I explored it I felt no surprise
      supposing the verdure to be the truth
            and daylight's monuments to be forgeries

There was the triumph of being there at all
At last
      and the transmogrified rock
            though more a wooded hill
                  still had not lost its identity

What luck!
Suddenly war *is* too important to be left to the generals!
And art too important to be left to the artists!
      someone hearing that
      someone following an ascent
            I must have heard it
                  else how would I know it?

The teacher teaching
      on a dangerous rock
And it might be the island called "Destruction"
            the one off Washington's coast

The irony thrilling
The dream and all its plots just thoughts

Oh, for a sandwich right now!
Even peanut butter and jelly
      high up an appetite
            even asleep it's all pretend

It's a Himalayan summit   a green refugia
Where to live in the afterlife alone
Yes, we can!
      hungry as birds and waving my arms

A visitor from the future who must see *all* the caves
Hug Point   Silver Point   and Ecola, too
Even the Jockey Cap is drilled
        white caps arriving out of the hat
                they emerge
                pour from the stone and weakness

See it happen from the highway to South Hemlock
South entrance to all that real estate can be
        hollow homes and shingled shacks
        cave dwellings all

I'm the boy that wandered away debt-free
Yet a person of interest
        still set on home invasion
                perhaps that ramshackle house in the forest
                half-collapsed

Surely shelter enough for an adventurous teenager
More a fallen treehouse than anything
"Click!"   take its picture   *belong* to it
        top secret

The boy watches the sea
The sea   the boy
        and we are a mutual authority
                so walk on the very edge of it
                the fringe of bubbles

The story of two identities that starts with bare feet
Sinking heel-first as the wave runs back
        remember?   *remember*?

The moats and buckets of the sandcastle crew
Intent on salty irrigation for the entire family
        awaiting the flood
                patient
                and proud of their work
                        in the bright, bright sun

The wet parapets are last-minute architecture
        before the surf's renovations are smoothly realized
                hopscotching the crenellated walls

Smiling oblivion!
End of a royal story
        the court must be brave
                for the tide's turned like a thorough investigation

Back of the beach
        the town's a collage of cut-and-paste resorts
Shiloh is one
        blue-and-white schematic
                the ocean in drag
A pattern of windows and habitat
Hyping the ancient world
                        as same-old-same-old

Be the kite flyer's proxy   a bird
Censored flight
        secrets too sacred for revelation
Air for dragon sticks and dragon tail
With a drum and flute to celebrate aloft
        the mystical feathered sky   lifting

There is no other Other
A fog-shining shore for a Wallace Stevens *tabula rasa*

A little girl is only four
Wave-jumping
        there at the sea's aprons and skirts
                thinly flung
                        the girl's dress blown back
Her mother attends
Her mother remembers wave-jumping

The sea is suddenly *purple*   *red*
And all the colors a fauvist imagines with ingenious love
And with those colors
        the mother and child adjourn the day
        and climb wooden stairs to backyard hammocks
                golden hearts to new delights

I'm penniless but full of belief
        a lot to worry about but not till later
The kelp there is seems a glistening bullwhip
They say it's algae but how can that be?

and what happened to the textbooks?

Well, it turns out algae's many different things
        including these rubbery strands
        lying all around
                draped and slippery-strange
We'll make a funeral for it   show respect

No one needed rescue
The lifeguard   jobless with binoculars
        looking for trouble down south
                in the direction of the Castle
Were any red flags flying?
Any calls for backup?
                no emergencies
                no climbers
                nobody even stomping on helpless barnacles

Watching the lifeguard watching
One man in all this sandy highway's lane
He's slightly tilted
        his binoculars at rest on the white wooden rail
There *is* something southerly but it's not an emergency

I asked him   like I'd asked the marine
Said to myself, "Go ahead!   take time…"

He wears a jerkin and he seems at ease
And he *must* be at ease in saving a life
Think of some hero's fictive intervention
        complete with critical acclaim
                for he has to discern
                out of all that background
                                what's not right

Life-and-death details
A crisis stirring in a distant crowd of waders
        he can tell hysteria
        the ocean's harm
Concentrates
        like a teacher studies wayward fingers
                and corrects
                as he would a foreign policy

More "spooky action at a distance"

I'll lifeguard a Chopin waltz
        and its treacherous *leggiero*
            "Slow practice, my friend!"
Those were his words once spoken to me

His ladder and tower and platform speech
Taught us to scan the page and save the composer for later

Be on the way to Chapman Bluff
To feed the gulls a loaf of borrowed bread
        and know what it means to not really know

Crumbs at your feet
        how close will they come to feast?
            how familiar will they be?
I know what I'll do!
I'll make it a bread *shower*
            the more bread   the more noise
                just like Wall Street

You know, they *never* get enough to eat
They're here with me   the darlings
        the terns too
And the closer they get the *bigger* they get
I never knew a simple seabird could seem so gigantic
        so clean

The bunch of them are flapping
            and fighting fights I started
Bad birds of the sea's second sight

Now that you're grown
        you allow
        that even juvenile delinquents need their calories
But what rudeness and "Me first!"
Still no one's died in the squabbling

It's just a convention of candidate gulls
And I am their glorious lobbyist
Have some more bread, bird patriots
        and tell me where your allegiance is

It's Alfred Hitchcock's flock
I'm ending hunger in the empty dunes and silky marram
     and it's bigger than politics
        they don't want to go
        I don't want to *see* them go

I feel my own pinfeathers starting
Recent history
     selfish opportunity flapping insanely
Wonder if they'll think of me
        somewhere over the Pacific
        think of the crusts of Wonder Bread

If they could pick me out of a flock of humans
My arms are open wide as yourselves
Back up in the sky
     are we finished, you and I?
     are we?
Retiring teenage birds

And a boy foxtrotting away to Infinity's bedrooms
A merry way of losing virginity
     with a Chinese translation of *Naked Lunch*
        breakfast and dinner
          barely listening
          for all the traffic of the foam

Thank you, Neptune!
Or do you prefer to be addressed as "Poseidon?"

You should know I greatly appreciate you
     and the little islands you make when the tide goes out

Those muddy ridges left
     all ripple-revealed
        and it's my desire to splash away
        until the tide turns back
Interim glee   more than nature intended
Familiar with every tidal detail
          as puddle master

The ocean's drawn a bath of inches in sand colored tan
Serenely transparent
     they are bodies of water like chameleon glass

Definitely too shallow for snorkeling!
Another giggle word for sure

And the little low tide islands are liquidating
With nothing left to lose of themselves
        so many miles of mud
                you'd think the tsunami's trough was at hand
                that something wasn't right

A worn out dream in the daytime with cars
Cars all over the ecology
        the birth of Earth Day
        screamin' 'n' cryin'
Black *box*cars en route to some commerce

Mister Short is driving the distance today
He's out there revving the Chevy again
        the new car never older than three short years
It's just not fair we cannot drive it!
Each of his *students*
        should drive his shiny machine!

But time is short
        it's going to get very wet around here
                and you'll close the book of tides and puddles' islands
Shivering in August
        to keyboard sonatas played to perfection

Margaritas in a bar
        with a beautiful girl from a wayward future
The drink with the salted rim
                                a synthetic brine

The brain is asleep again
A book's for sale   somewhere civic
Fast-forward the beach
        to a time and date right out of astrology

And it's loud in the lounge
And all that's left of age thirteen
        swirls in a long-stem
                the drink as common as generic Margaret
You just don't know the sequel alone together

Suppose the alcohol is liquid amnesia
        why do this to the misting stars?
                their eclipse by stone?
                        why do this to the teacher?
What celebration more billboard than exhilaration?

It is brakes   this bar   this sadness
True love's a funeral in search of mourners
        swaying under the influence
Motorcycles having usurped the silent Schwinn
            alcohol all around
            yet belonging to no one

That a boy is going nowhere he belongs
                    accepting the offer of a drink
Then how overthrown is the virgin mind!
What would have made you make a face
        and make you say,
        "How can you drink this stuff?"

It was H.D. Moe's "burning snow, burning snow"
        what he'd say in the year 6,000
                for *that* was the year he said he was writing for

I'd be beyond the green flash of the sun's last light
        above the ocean
                that's now a word you whisper
                eyes closed and caressed
And dressed to kill the conscience over and over
Sadly getting lost

Break through to what was
        and cannot be destroyed or laid siege to
Drift back   like the gulls
To Haystack
        to preeminence
                belonging to a faith of miles away
Reverse fermentation

Retreat to backstage and backlit rehearsal
Be kind again
        as you were wont to be to your new best friend
And that song's unsuspecting lyrics

Love it again
 recalling the dreams yet to be explained
Including the one in which *somebody*
  perhaps yourself
   hid behind dunes
   waiting there as if trying to be hidden

Waiting there the way it's fun to hide away
Secretly removed to secret dunes
  staring long distances
   most of the way to Hawaii
    with just a tickle of agoraphobia

Still thinking salvation's out there if only we are vigilant
And knowing the names of the next millennium's leaders
  spiritual and otherwise

Waiting in the observatory sand
All of golf's bunker traps brought together
  outsmarting the search party
  who learn too slowly to find the ball
     or anything at all

Watch the beach
Watch the world
  an onlooker child left to honest appraisal
I'll be the observer on no particular assignment
  delving into ideas of space beyond the sandbox
  and the spiritual canasta of a beige playpen

Be not in a nightmare longer
Let it be this good dream of hiding out
  courageous
   returned to a crescent concealment
   so sacred
    it's outside in

Watch the show
It's a planet a wanderer
  like Venus
  and Mars
   and Altair IV
We'll wander on this
    our wandering world

And once the vigil's over
        be your most eloquent self
                the muse of all the seascape coast
Be still and look a long way off
As if that distance comprised some critical thought
                        sustained by a pedal
                a soundboard
                        and sympathetic strings

Like the blur of the zither played
        while the credits rolled
                The Third Man walking
Lost in the same sub-atomic dilemma
        that short-circuited Robby
        who'd been ready, willing and able to fight the Id
                save for a built-in constraint

For he could not harm any rational being
And Morbius was also the Id monster!

Lay low just in case you are a monster too
Things may end this way
        without makeup
                the last time the clocks are wound
                with a shared conviction
Lugubrious   lost even then

There was always a little of this in going away
Where is that same ordinary day?
Kick the snake if it shows up
        illicit   Freudian
                there is sin
                the soft sand is for kneeling
In its pews may the prayers be questions' gestures

Attention is paid
I turned to the unobvious island
        the smaller one
        between the lighthouse and the headland
Close to the well-watered shore it was

I'd tell my sister I saw it there
Like a stationary rocky whale

while I was still a child
        married to the money of the moment

Tide that will last as long as lessons Chopin taught
        tubercular   perfumed
The famous daguerreotype brightens
He too is sleepless
            with harmony

There are handwritten notations
        some trick of the light
                sci-fi without permission

The little reef like an oceanic domino
Indifferent to all the turning
        of the Fresnel lens
        and my own distracted gazing

Pure power's heavy gift of waters
Midway to my twenties
        an emerald inset in August
            and a temperate zone's white tower

Stone as a conception of the sixteenth century
A detail of an oil canvas
Write it down that the story's ended out to sea
        its phrases dancing beyond the plot

All the hills have finished with their height above
        being lines on the level leaving now with shoes

Pretend the ragged rock's a casket with nothing to preserve
Or a ship turned to stone
            with reverberation
A door to the cellars of the sea
And you think how well was all this world made wild!

Two years after there'd be a bus ride from Portland
Solo remembrance
        and every two years in August
        I'd return to see if everything's there
            and it's all okay

Return to walk lightly again

retrace
revisit
It was a vow to do this even if I became a senator
Return   reenact
Take a bus to the beach bewitched

Use Eisenhower's highways
        belonging to the road just beyond the curvature
The way to stay a boy and stay mid-century
Get 1957 right before moving on

A bus through the Tillamook Burn
        Cottage Grove
                and the rest of the way
                        through manicured forests
                                brambles
                                and briared pastures

Cannon Beach Junction
Exclusive   alone
Already making ancient two summers ago
        the melancholy coming along
        coming into town as if it were a past life
                its lucid dream

The friendly bus driver
        perhaps a little curious about his eager passenger
                positioned well-forward
                to see the one-at-a-time towns coming and going
                        the front seat taken

All alone with limited dollars
        hear the "shush" of the Greyhound's door
        opening and closing
                an acoustic compartment's roar
And then you enter the outdoors of downtown

Still uncrowded as before

There are jobs if you could stay
Jobs in spite of "Auld Lang Syne"
        the song that puts a period to a timespan

There's construction

Bright two-by-fours
        amidst old money's shingled gray
And there seems to be room
                for new wooden skeletons
                to end up optimistic pioneer

So I went past houses others own
And pretended other families had taken me in
        an exchange student sent by a certain marine
                on reconnaissance
                in sea neighborhoods
Down-climbing stairs to the soft, soft sand

Be a planetary ghost
        whose haunted home is hereabouts
                amidst the rhetoric of locals
A young president of all the ether
When a sudden sun has warmed the cracked gray benches

Thinking of Nemo   Captain Nemo
En route to his island base
Would he have had some leagues left over
        to travel   submerged
                and see the *sunken* monolith
                that hidden Haystack said to be out there somewhere?

A rock included in his reckoning

Oceanography will say just where it may be
Just play for time
        and secrets may be told
                as part of your peace of mind
                holding steady   unseen
                        a stone construction of the mind

Return every two years for a lifetime
Two, because it's the *only* even-numbered prime number
Two *also* because it harbors duality
        and black-and-white must be obeyed

Return with friends   best friends
Like the singer
        senior week
                in the pause before commencement

Fred and I deciding on Seaside from Cannon
The hike to be accomplished with apples only
        so that we were starving our way
        past Tillamook Head

Both of us in need of a teacher more than ever before
And we tried the cliffs like the stock market
        the surf zone the loudest sound you ever heard
        our hearts aslant with determination

We were threading once-upon-a-time trees
The trail   accidentally taken
        and the lighthouse as near as it would ever appear

Both of us so tired the town of Seaside would not let us in
As we staggered block by block to a burger joint
        Fred had to wait for me to catch up
We were two Britishers in wartime Burma
                on the verge of beriberi

After we came back to life
And were no longer famished
        some guy in a pickup
        darkly indifferent
                returned us to trailhead
                to Cannon Beach

And later   Gary
A companion from the universe of elementary school
        eventually coming
                half-blind and broken-hearted
                        to Silver Point
                        to Ecola's bluff
                                and Indian Beach

He would see and hear what he could of the place
His wife with blankets and pillows

"Are you comfy?   can I get you something, honey?"

Saw for himself
        what his best friend had alleged
                was all the comfort there could ever be

                sitting by the sea
This precious sea so long recited

The recital a concert
The concert a continuance
                      what does this do?

The eyes are windows
You live in a house of bones
      and belong to a faith of marrow and miles

The teacher will teach me
      to play outside the sandbox
We will crisscross together all that terrain
"Be *careful*, Stevie," he'd say
"Practice slowly!"

He, quoting Isidor Philipp
The blurb beneath the frontispiece of his technique book:
"Practice with patience and *always* with patience"

He would clip articles   show evidence
What Rubenstein had to say   and Horowitz
      proof that what *he* told me to do was echoed elsewhere
      the greats brought to bear
        the interviews made to matter

There were trills to master
              arpeggios and scales
There was the art of the octaves
The art of thirds, sixths and even sevenths
      all of it to be learned and *relearned*

Whatever you could stretch and barely reach
The choice of fingers
      the use of weight to create the tone
        and the *singing* tone was always best

There was the constant mystery of how much pedal to use
      whether to use *any*
The honor system employed
You were simply to tell the truth
        you'd practiced
        or you'd merely played

Or did nothing and followed household pets around

You might roll a chord
Or strike it   all the notes of the chord at once
You had to guard against cold hands
        on recital days
        at his house on Lake Washington

But his master stroke was Cannon Beach
That instruction
        and acquaintance with power
                that was his studio and all pedagogy
                the whole course
                        and graduation, too

It was like the study of a grand composition
Far past the pages I'd known till then
        as if it were the keys to repertoire itself

Makes you very tired just *thinking* of it
Good-tired
        exhausted the way Fred and I were
                after the amazing journey to Seaside
Weary as close calls can make you

Just as the teacher took his students to concerts
So he brought us to Oregon
        to thanatopsis
                and a pastel theater of forbidden sound

The domestic shore still a foreign planet's place
Where Krell musicians serenade the sea life
        all the creatures in *Between Pacific Tides*

Gail Mitchell's "Talk Story"
        in a children's book made of basalt
                hugely open
An accidental drawing from life

And from Ecola State Park
A picture taken
        black-and-white
        chosen for brochures

and showing mid-century long distance

Let's talk about that
We can talk about *anything*, right?
Talk about how mysterious was the scene southwards
        shades of gray with a blue psychology
                blue *implied*

A better portrait of the shore than what the rainbow paints

And the photo seemed a camera's pan
Grayly expressive
        the foreground
                the background
A seascape of missing children
                how ghosts see things

Whatever text it had was subsumed in that faraway
Chapman Bluff
        the Bird Rocks
                and beyond them   Haystack
The whole a presentation of solitude
A melancholy counting years as seconds

The nearby trees making a triptych and more
The wings of spruce and cedar
        attest to a perspective
                the result of an interview with Chopin
                who makes a case for Ecola's height

It's a daguerreotype far from Paris salons
                tapestry and clock-death
And viewing this picture brought silence to silence
The pauses between Hoffmann's Tales
        also French

It was the future I saw seeing anything at all
The inaccessible *canceled* future
        that which thirteen years can never know

Next time
The next time, *believe* me
        the ocean barely accompanied
        for thought alone had overthrown

It may be a city overtakes this surrender

"It's going to be good!"
        my mother had promised at 4am
                and it *was* good
                as in Genesis
The eight corners of the world in one western place
As blue as a broken marriage
Such sadness as empty seascapes require

Space as separation
        belonging to a faith of miles and miles
        and preternaturally clear

It is surgical
        the way the camera
                has excised the sense of that afternoon
Sundowning by degrees of gray-pearly

You have a knowledge of one day's eternity
Quiet as all its timeout says
        in quintessential serenity
                monk moment
                the acolyte's first meditation!

Monastery of one boy only
No rice or ritual staring as yet

"It's going to be good…"
        between trees
                the middle distance told
                and retold in the telling
Micro to macro

At Hug Point   low tide
The spectacle of light green encroaching
        upleaping as sea lettuce
        leaping the walls volcanic
                a mural of pastel flames
                in the midst of the tiniest barnacles ever made!

The gallery is there
Olfactory   feathery   embroidered walls of the sea
        as detailed as it wants to be

More instruction!

Everywhere is Nature teaching!
Bright scenery backstage
        the set is set in motion
                a *museum* it is
Art under oath saying we are innocent until proven adult

The ocean's a graffiti surprise and tag tournament

The last night
        the teacher and his students promised to appear
                on stage for sentencing
But we danced our way to beach fires
Just to be in their swirl of sparks
                        part-fog and part-smoke

Bonfires prior to rules and signs
Hearths gone outside
        Siegfried's furnaces signaling Wagner
        music in another way
And orange disguised as a prehistoric color

The forests' first tasks
                before books and journals
                before the northwest totems
The wood-drifted pyre

Incinerated love for the glass sea's movie loop
The logs outgassing fleet fairies
Those sparks as mentors to starlight's stars

Towards the one thought!
Ancestral
        holding an orange finale
        with yellow as well
                        almost formal

Hands and feet for the heat
The entire cannon melted deep down
All the shore's black circles
        taut with aphelion   perihelion
                to the hearths!

We were becalmed with embers
Melancholy's antithesis
          all the fires' bright engines!

Say "Tolovana" once more
And remember a party
          and "To your health!"
               the strongest we would ever be
               you and I

A party   a Tolovana social
What Socialism reaches for but never grasps
          that upright piano at the edge of the crowd
          like a happy ending deferred
               its keyboard and pedals awaiting a proposal

Years after and beyond recollection
I would start seeing you to make myself go away
          what politics never is:
          true love

A party of the future
Where instruments remind us of music
          and we try to decide what's important
               some distance towards a church
               becalmed with catholic wafers

It took time away
          in a swirl of conversations so urgent
               it seemed the world waited just outside the door

The party was like a radio's nighttime blur
Words from ornate mahogany
          the family room's dialed centerpiece
The world going to sleep
Or waking up to sound track and testament

Tolovana relatives with a wish to adopt

Then came the dream of a cabin
Perhaps a rental while I'm still a young kid
          one room   one night

The Brothers Grimm took the money

the last of the allowance
They served ginger bread for breakfast
The cabin was made of solitude's timbers and too many crimes

An honor to stay there   welcome-safe
A dream's *inner* dream and sanctum
        from which you wake twice
                your only instrument
                a pitch pipe for *a capella* carols
                        summer notwithstanding

Cannon Beach transformed yet again
As if Bruegel had been by
        and you must enter the painting
                before it dries to nothing in particular

Shadow beach that plays tag with the daytime
The little house
        built for thirteen years of life so far
        where Clarke's *Childhood's End* is duly postponed
And one-way time's arrested

Again the lighthouse
This time engulfed by a perfect rogue wave
        spreading wings of itself with the shock of attack

Is this for you?
Is this your oceanic angel's appearance?
Train yourself to see it
        rare as a war situation resolved with seraphim
What we would think of past science and prisons

I saw a caravan coming
        winding down from the uplands of Tillamook
Psychology a part of its patient train
Empathic   the guests of nomads

Their traveling classroom
        exchange students from all that was and may well be

And recognition came with each arrival
Friends   a favorite uncle
        movie stars
        especially cowboys and cowgirls

It could have been Shelley's entourage
The procession from "The Triumph of Life"

Mister Short   my teacher with second sight
        sees an adjusted Haystack
                with multipled pinnacles
                        countless   near-shore and shining
                                uncanny

Other crowds came
Perhaps the history of all visitations simultaneously made
And all the fashions since Sacagawea
        wanting interpretation
        wanting the same attention
                as young pianists give to the study of Mozart

It was an *operatic* crowd
        that said,
                "Why don't we stay here
                in case the story of the world has ended?"

That story to include the dream of an elevator
        inside a Haystack Hotel
                                and super-secret
A fortress stocked with Kelloggs Corn Flakes
All the floors were stone

You rode the elevator up to the birds
        to be a lookout for a tunneled Gibraltar
                supplied with popcorn
                and an old Philco TV
                                test patterned

There were hallways inside
And one led to a Krell laboratory
I was Flash Gordon caught up in alien intrigue
        the honeycombed basalt a comfort zone
        because nobody knows that anyone's home

Unless it's James Cagney, Jr.
James could be trusted and told
        and fifty years later he *would* be told
                an awful lot *more*, too
                walking this beach as did my teacher

And I listened to James as well
On the same brilliant shore that was like a lending institution
        Bank of Summer   big   beautiful

"Make it stop!" he'd say
And I'd say the same thing to him
        our little joke when life got a little too interesting!
We *both* said it *apropos* great beauty
                    that was somehow unbearable

Now I saw him again with the others
But there was something wrong with the ocean
It was still the ocean and the boy watching each other
        and not knowing what the other may do

Yet there'd been a tremendous shaking that went on and on
Meaning only one thing
        and sure enough
                though the ocean was quiet
                the water was retreating!
                                to *way* out there!

We all knew what that meant
And someone said it was behaving like the Indian Ocean
        that Christmas of '04
        when the earthquake summoned the sea to flood

Yes, it was a tsunami's drawing back before the runup
And a piano that stood in the sinking sand
That Steinway   was doomed

"Higher ground, everyone!"
"Evacuate *now*!"
"It's coming!"

No question   no doubt
The sea's gone bye-bye beyond the second Needle
        gone past everything
        the greatest minus since 1700
                when the last megathust occurred!

It was beyond a tide table's powers to add or subtract
And   dream or not

I knew that now I should go
     in the trough's extremity go
     to the far side   the sea cave
                    and hurry!

"Steve!! what are you *doing*?!"
"The wave is coming, the *wave*!"

"It's okay!   there's time!   just enough!
I'm halfway there!   I'll be all right!
    see you later on the moral high ground!
    Don't worry!!"

"Steve! come *back*!!"

Dream or waking state I just couldn't say
But I'd round the great monolith of Haystack Rock alone
    thanks to the tsunami's temporary gift of extra beach
Where the great Pacific had never let us go!

Running like the horses!
Running closer across the strange damp desert
    deep brown with kelp
    and stranded fish
        my heart belonging to all of it
        and the rest of me, too!

Running on the seafloor with *just* enough time
There's the sea cave at last!
The backside entrance found!

If it's a dream I will not drown
If it's not I won't care!

About the Author

I was born in Massachusetts. I had two wonderful sisters. I loved the east coast's seasons and I missed them when my father took a job with Boeing and the whole family headed for Seattle. My mother had bought a piano for me and I loved every day I could play it — nothing else could hold my attention.

Later, high school was okay, but I daydreamed through a year and a half of the University of Washington and later dropped out of Willamette University in Salem; I was just too restless. A visit to Colorado resulted in a lifelong love of the square states of the west and whenever possible I find some excuse to hit the road.

In the nineties I made friends with writers in San Francisco and grew to love the poetry chaos that happened and spread into the next century…so it's Mozart piano sonatas and scribbling. I owe any good luck I've had to my partner Loie Johnson whose kindly nature means everything to me. Special thanks to my close friends, Richard Loranger, Jan Steckel, Glenn Ingersoll, Mel C. Thompson, John Rowe, James Cagney, Jr., Richard Hack, Mary-Marcia Casoly, Joe Petolino, Dale Jensen, Judy Wells, Bonnie Landfield, Tim Xonnelly, Jane Green and my excellent publisher, Deborah Fruchey! -— love to all!

Other Books by This Author

Other Books by Last Laugh Productions

The Nearest Place Distant, by Stephen Francis Cosgrove

Hint, by Deborah L. Fruchey

Shattered Windows, by Deborah L. Fruchey

Eye Masks, by Rudy Jon Tanner

What Still Matters, by Johanna Ely

We'll Always Have Stockton, by Steve Arntson

The Worlds According to Loki, 2nd Edition, by Vampyre Mike Kassel

For Whoever Thinks a Piano is Furniture, by Rudy Jon Tanner

The Hall of Painted Sonnets, Sonnets by Steve Arntson, Art by Diane Lee Moomey

Embodied (hardcover), by Jan Dederick

Gypsy & Other Poems, by Steve Arntson

Armageddon Bootcamp...and other poems (hardcover), by Maria Elizabeth Rosales

Three Kinds of Dark (ebook, hardcover), by Deborah L. Fruchey

Touchstones (hardcover), by Maria Elizabeth Rosales

Priestess of Secrets, by Deborah L. Fruchey

Bat Flower: poems, plays & other perversions, by Vampyre Mike Kassel

Armadillo (ebook, hardcover), by Deborah L. Fruchey

Color Cards & Self Healing, by Jean Luo

A Scandalous Creature, by Deborah L. Fruchey

Mental Illness Ain't for Sissies, by Deborah L. Fruchey

The Unwilling Heiress, by Deborah L. Fruchey

www.lastlaughproductions.org

www.ingramcontent.com/pod-product-compliance
Lightning Source LLC
Chambersburg PA
CBHW081357270326
41930CB00015B/3336